HEY, I'M ANITA

A fun-loving chilled out Kiwi who fell in love with travelling and purchased her first one-way ticket at 19. I have been travelling full-time since 2012 and decided to create a travel blog to show the world the different countries, and cultures from around the world.

In 2016 my blog gained huge success and it became my full-time job. Travelling the world and writing about it is my passion.

Travel for me has been more educational than all my school years combined. I find travel not only an incredible learning experience but it gives me compassion, it gives me gratitude and I get to meet some of the most interesting people around the world!

My passion is to inspire others to get out there and see the world, particularly the lesser-known destinations like Albania. I also want to inspire solo females that want to travel but don't feel like they can do it alone. I promise you it will be one of the most amazing experiences you will ever have in your life. Solo travel teaches confidence and makes you enjoy your own company!

Enjoy the guide and let me know how you like it!

Anita Hendrieka

TRAVEL BLOGGER

WWW.ANITAHENDRIEKA.COM

CONTENTS

CONTENTS

Albania

As Albania's tourism is increasing rapidly, the demand for information is increasing too.

Tourism is still relatively new in Albania so it can be hard to find actual information that's helpful for your trip there. If you come across information online, it's usually from other bloggers who have visited the country for a week and can't give you the in-depth information you really need.

Therefore, I have created this full Albania travel guide with all the information you need to visit Albania for the first time or find the hidden gems if you have been living here already! Albania is full of beautiful surprises. I have lots of great information for you to use during your travels to Albania.

I have lived in Albania since 2017, so I have a great knowledge of the do's and don'ts and the best local spots to visit and the ones you should avoid!

I also feel like I have a great local insight as my boyfriend is Albanian and is a video content creator. We together explore beautiful places around the country and try our hardest to capture the spots that no one has ever captured on film before.

After writing and promoting Albania for years, I noticed that many travellers who come, don't get to explore the most beautiful spots, and that's because they don't know about them! My mission is to change that.

How to get to Albania

Albania can be reached in many ways from air, bus and ferry.

FLYING TO ALBANIA

There are two airports in Albania, Kukes airport and Tirana International Airport, which is the main airport in the country. There is another currently being built in Vlora which is set to be finished by approximately 2025.

Flights in and out of Tirana are usually expensive. The airport is owned by a private company that control the prices and availability.

Wizz Air, Lufthansa, Air Albania and Air Serbia are some of the main airlines that currently run in and out of Tirana.

OVERLAND FROM GREECE

You can easily catch a bus from Athens to Saranda. It takes about 9 hours and costs around €35. It's not necessarily a comfortable trip as it's long and usually full, but flights in and out of Athens are much more frequent and affordable than in Albania usually.

You can also catch a bus from Ioannina which stops at Gjirokastër from there you can catch a bus elsewhere in Albania.

FERRY FROM GREECE

Another way which is incredibly easy is catching a ferry from Corfu! The Island of Corfu is only a 30-minute ferry ride from Saranda. Prices and timetables depend on the season.

Corfu does direct flights to a bunch of other European countries. If I want to fly to the UK I will fly out of Corfu as EasyJet do cheap and direct flights from there!

This can be a great way to get to Albania with a quick stopover in Corfu. Usually, you will have to stay in Corfu the night depending on when your flight is but it's a good excuse to explore the island as it's very beautiful too.

OVERLAND FROM MONTENEGRO

If you're coming from Montenegro there are buses between Kotor and Podgorica going to Shkodër and Tirana. If you want to head towards the south, you will have to change buses in Tirana.

OVERLAND FROM MACEDONIA

There are usually multiple buses from Skopje to Tirana. Please check with your accommodation that these are still the times that the bus leaves.

BOAT FROM ITALY

You can catch a boat from Durres to Bari and Ancona. There are several crossings per week but it's best to contact the ferries themselves as crossings and prices change from month to month.

RECENT HISTORY

Albania's history is beyond fascinating compared to some other countries in the world. From 1941 to 1992 **Albania was under the strict communist rule of the leader Enver Hoxha**. Everything was controlled, from food to housing and jobs.

Some compare it to North Korea, but only those who lived through communism will know. There were labour camps where political prisoners were sent if they said something that the communist leader did not like. **The prisoners built the infrastructure that Albania sees today**.

After the collapse of communism, Albania saw itself as a democracy.

Unfortunately, **in 1997 the government collapsed after a dodgy pyramid scheme.** Over 2/3rds of the population invested their life savings into this scheme which meant most people lost everything they had worked hard for all those years.

The civil unrest saw a lot of anger and violence from the citizens of Albania, many fled from the country for a better life.

The civil unrest went on for 6 months and when visiting Albania, **you will see for yourself that Albania is still recovering to this day.**

There is still a lot of corruption within government sectors today. **The difference between Albania and many other countries is that corruption is right in front of you and no one is really hiding it.**

Ancient History

Have you heard of the Illyrians?

Many only discuss communism and the civil unrest as the history of Albania but the real history dives way older than that. If you move to Albania, you will find yourself in many conversations with locals about ancient Albania and the Illyrians whom many believe are the same/ older than the ancient Greeks.

There is so much that hasn't been uncovered and publicized about Albania's ancient history.

The ancient site of Apollonia which is in Fier and is a popular site to see if anyone who loves ancient history, is less than 5% excavated.

Many archaeological sites in Albania have been dug a fraction and left to fend for themselves.

Unfortunately, a lot of the time there just isn't the funding to continue digging.

One of the biggest ancient graves was found near Korca in 2018 which archaeologist believe are more than 5000 years old!

I will tell you about some of the best archaeological sites in Albania within this guide!

Albanian Language

Shqip is one of the most fascinating languages I have come across and one of the hardest to learn (in my eyes!). It's an Indo-European language that **relates to no other language in the world,** it has its own roots.

The North and South speak different dialects. In the south they speak Tosk, and, in the north, they speak Gheg.

The younger generation in Albania mostly knows some English as they are taught in school. The older generation you will find speak none such as the adorable Albanian grandmothers.

You don't have to worry about the language barrier when you travel to Albania as you can always get past it with some English and some hand gestures.

If you really want to impress the locals when you come to Albania it's a great idea to learn a few words. **They love it when people try and speak their language.** It's always met with a smile and a little giggle. Luckily for you, I have put together Shqip bingo, on the next page!

Shqip Bingo

How many Albanian words can you use during your time in Albania?!

01 Përshëndetje – **Hello**	02 Faleminderit - **Thank you**	03 Gazuar – **Cheers or Salut!**	04 Mirëmëngjes! -**Good morning!**	05 Po- **Yes**
06 Jo - **No**	07 Natën e mirë! - **Good night!**	08 Mirupafshim **Good bye!**	09 Më falni - **Excuse me**	10 anglisht - **English**
11 Mirëmbrëma! **- Good evening**	12 Te lutem! - **You're welcome**	13 Unë quhem ... - **My name is**	14 një **- one**	15 dy - **two**
16 tre - **three**	17 katër - **four**	18 pesë - **five**	19 gjashtë - **six**	20 shtatë **- seven**
21 tetë **- eight**	22 nëntë **- nine**	23 dhjetë **- ten**	24 Mirë - **Good**	25 Keq - **Bad**
26 Shume mire - **very good**	27 Sa lekë - **How much Lek?**	28 Bukur - **Beautiful**	29 Birrë - **Beer**	30 Verë - **Wine**

Facts about Albania

Albania is a fascinating place with many interesting daily routines and cultural facts. From my local friends and extended family, I have learnt so many interesting facts about Albanian culture and history, and some of the daily rituals that people do here and now I want to share them with you!

1. NO MEANS YES, AND YES MEANS NO

When talking to an Albanian you may notice that it looks like they are disagreeing with you, but they nod their heads in the opposite direction than those of us from western cultures.

Shake your head up and down and that means no, shake it side to side and that means yes. The only other place that I know that does the headshake the opposite way is India! This is one of those Albanian facts that can take awhile to get used to, but if you do, it might be super confusing once you go back home!

2. ALBANIANS HAVE STRONG BELIEFS

I love learning new facts about Albanian culture and beliefs because they are very interesting and different to those I grew up with in New Zealand. For example, you may notice when walking around residential areas that on the fence or entrance of the houses there are teddy bears or dolls. This is to ward off any bad spirits. Another belief is if a liquid like a drink is spilt then you must pour water over that spill to ward off bad luck.

Also, if you order a second raki from a café you may notice they will bring it in a new glass but pour the raki into the glass you're already using. Apparently, if you are given a new glass then it means you get a new partner. There are many other fascinating Albanian beliefs that many of them live by too!

3. RELIGION WAS BANNED IN ALBANIA

One of the most interesting facts about Albania is that during the communist era (1941 to 1992) religion was outright banned making Albania the first atheist country in the world.

Many mosques and churches were burned down during the Enver Hoxha ruling. Nowadays, Albania is known as one of the most tolerant countries when it comes to religion. People from all religions live together peacefully here.

4. MORE ALBANIANS LIVE OUTSIDE OF ALBANIA THAN INSIDE

The population of Albania is 2.8 million but because it's hard to find work and conditions are poor here, there are more Albanians living outside of Albania. In fact, around 10 million Albanians live abroad. After the fall of communism and the collapse of the economy, it saw the largest emigration movement in Europe since World War 2.

Many Albanians settled in Greece and Italy along with Switzerland, Germany and Turkey. For many here, the dream is to live outside of Albania and find work with better pay conditions and a chance to further their career or study.

5. THERE WERE OVER 750,000 BUNKERS SCATTERED AROUND THE COUNTRY

During the communist era, Enver Hoxha demanded that over 750,000 bunkers be built for an upcoming war. But in fact, that was all a lie and the bunkers were built for no real reason. You will find over 160,000 of them scattered throughout Albania still today. Some have been turned into farming sheds, artists' studios and even hotels. The only time they were partially used was during the civil war, which was in 1997.

6. THE CAR OF CHOICE IS MERCEDES

Just about everyone here drives a Mercedes. The reason? After the mass emigration of Albanians leaving everyone started bringing back Mercedes Benz.

They are reliable cars and perfect for the poor roads that are here in Albania. Now having a Mercedes is a must-have for many. Most of them come from Germany and are perfectly legal.

The Albanians have a sort of entrepreneurial sense as every time they would go back home to Albania after working in another country, they would bring a Mercedes to sell. This is how the whole country is now full of old Mercedes Benz!

7. THERE'S NO MCDONALDS IN ALBANIA

Don't expect to find a big mac on your travels to Albania! That's right, there is no McDonalds in sight. McDonald's haven't even bothered trying to come to Albania as there would be a huge cultural push back on the idea. Albanians are more interested in coffee shops. The idea of having a fast-food chain like McDonald's coming into their country is horrifying to most. There is, however, a wannabe McDonald's in Tirana called Kolonat.

8. XHIRO – AN ALBANIAN TRADITION

One of Albania's tradition is called Xhiro. Early in the evening Albanians will leave their homes and go for a walk down the main road of wherever they live. This is a good chance to catch up with everyone. Sometimes the farmers will come and sell their products or people will start little BBQs on the side of the street.

9. CODE OF BESA

Safety in Albania is a question I get asked again and again but there is nothing to worry about here. The code of Best is a very old cultural practice in Albania, which roughly translates to 'word of honour' or 'to keep the promise'. To them, this means that Albanians have a code of honour to look after those who need help.

10. ALBANIANS LOVE AN ESPRESSO

Like most of the Balkans, they are huge coffee lovers. You will notice the art of chilling in a café, catching up with friends over an espresso is prominent.

There are an insane amount of coffee shops in Albania. I even started drinking espressos after I moved here just to fit in and experience true Albanian culture.

11. 70% OF THE COUNTRY IS MOUNTAINOUS TERRAIN

Even though a lot of people come to the country to visit the Albanian Riviera, in fact, most of the country is mountainous landscape. Because of this perception that Albania is full of beaches, one of the most surprising facts about Albania for many visitors is that 70% of the country is mountains and the average elevation here is 708 metres (2,323 ft) above sea level.

In the north, you will find the most amazing hikes and trekking routes which I do talk about in this guide.

12. THEIR LANGUAGE IS UNLIKE NO OTHER

Albanian or 'Shqip' is such a unique language. If you look at the etymology behind the language it is an Indo-European language.

There are two dialects, one being Tosk (the southern dialect) and the other Gheg (the northern dialect). It's a hard language to learn for almost everyone as it has no 'cousin' languages.

13. THEY HAVE SIESTAS!

This is one of my favourite facts about Albanian culture and one I was happy to adopt! During the hottest part of the day 2 pm-6 pm, most shops will close to have a sort of siesta!

This is not so apparent in the likes of Tirana but more so in cities like Saranda and villages throughout the country.

During this time Albanian's will relax and take some time out to drink coffee or do nothing whatsoever.

CULTURAL NORMS

<u>Staring:</u> In Albania, it's totally normal and encouraged to stare. You may find at the start it might be a bit uncomfortable, but you will have to get used to it!

I have had old men stop in the middle of the street to just stare at me. Nowadays I just try and laugh and give a good old stare back!

<u>Expressing:</u> Albanians are very expressive. They love to move their hands when they talk.

Albanians can also be very loud when they are talking if I'm comparing to my country of New Zealand. Most of the time they are just having a conversation but sound like they are arguing.

<u>The headshake:</u> In some parts of Albania, they will shake their head side to side for a yes and up and down for a no.

They also shake their head side to side when they are listening in a conversation. It can get very confusing, especially if you're asking a question and the answer is yes but their head is saying something else.

<u>Grunting:</u> Upon my observations, while living in Albania, I have noticed that Albanians grunt a lot.

In fact, I have listened to a whole conversation of an old man answering a phone with just grunting and noises instead of words. It's safe to say that was the highlight of the week.

<u>Honest communication:</u> If you want to know about how your weight is doing, ask an Albanian. Don't be offended if Albanians say that you look thin or fat.

Weight is not something that's a taboo subject to them. I still struggle with this if I'm honest. Although, when I'm having a skinny day, it's the best confidence boost.

Dress: You're welcome to wear whatever you like during your time in Albania. The women make a big effort when it comes to dressing up.

They love to wear big high heels and dresses that I would only wear once in my lifetime, to the local club. I always feel underdressed at a club or sometimes even walking down the street. Albanian women have great style.

The older generation of men usually wear suits, yes suits! Just for having a coffee.

You may notice that most of the older women in Albania are wearing all black. There is a reason for this. This is to pay respects to loved ones that have passed. They usually wear black for as long as 10-20 years after that person has passed away.

Greetings: Albanians will usually greet you with a kiss on each cheek or a handshake.

When older women greet younger women, you will normally get a million kisses, a pinch on the cheek and squeezed until you can't breathe.

Dating: Some families still arrange marriage but nowadays this not common at all. Sometimes the family will be open to their son/daughter dating a foreigner. I have only heard from one girl I met that it was a problem for her, and she wasn't accepted into the family.

From personal experience, I have an Albanian boyfriend and his family have welcomed me like I'm their daughter.

However, dating is not really something that Albanians do. But saying that, if you're looking for an Albanian boyfriend you will easily find one.

If a single man goes out with a single woman, it's usually considered that they are together. So, ladies, if you do go to dinner with a man make it clear that you want to get to know each other and going for dinner doesn't mean you're boyfriend and girlfriend.

Men generally don't like women who have dated many other men in that city/town too. A woman is especially off-limits if she has been with anyone that you are friendly with.

Albanian men will do anything for their girls and can usually be quite possessive. Most will get jealous easily if you do have guy friends. Don't take offence to this though, it just means they care and they will openly tell you that. I have heard the same about Albanian women too.

Gender roles: Albanian women generally look after the house and the men work for the family.

This is how most families work in Albania but today it's now common for women to be working too. Gender roles are still very much prominent in Albanian society.

As unemployment in Albania is very high, a lot of men will sit in coffee shops for much of the day.

Albanian flexy time: If someone says to meet at a particular time it usually means at least half an hour after that. Sometimes it's even considered polite to be late.

Even Dr/dentist appointments are merely suggestions. No wonder nothing gets done in Albania quickly.

Albanians don't like commitment so arranging things ahead of time probably won't end well. Take it from experience.

SUPERSITITIONS

Albanians have many interesting beliefs, many that you probably have never come across before. Let me tell you about some Albanian superstitions!

➡If you have finished a glass of raki and you order another, the waiter will pour the raki into the cup you are already using. They will never give you a new cup. This is because if you change the cup, you change lovers!

➡You may notice stuffed toys hanging outside houses/apartments. This is to ward off bad spirits. People also hang garlic outside their homes or restaurants for the same reason.

➡ Never cut your fingernails and leave them on the ground because whoever steps on them will fight with you. Be careful!

➡ When you enter a new place that you have never been to, you should enter with your right foot otherwise it's bad luck.

➡If you have bread you need to throw out you should kiss it 3 times before putting it in the bin.

➡ Don't midnight snack because it's bad luck. *My boyfriend definitely doesn't abide by this superstition.*

➡If you spill coffee you're going to get money!

➡ You should blow on your hands every time you touch a gland otherwise an illness will get worse.

➡If you spill wine you have to pour water over it otherwise there will be blood spilt next time.

➡ If you leave a spoon full of food left on your plate the whole meal will not give you energy.

➡ If your hands are cold you're being honest.

➡ Do not whistle at night it's bad luck!

Health & Safety

Is Albania safe? This is the top question I get asked again and again now that I live in Albania. For many people, the only understanding of an Albanian is the actors who play the bad guys in the movie Taken. This country is a lot safer than any other European country I have visited, however.

Albania seems to be hugely misunderstood. **The last unrest in Albania was in 1997 after civil unrest broke out when a government pyramid scheme failed, and many Albanian families lost everything. In terms of conflict against others, Albania has not been in any since WW2.**

As a tourist, I have been living in Albania since 2017 so I think I have a good grasp of safety here. I haven't had one incident of feeling unsafe and I have not been in any trouble at all here. In fact, it's been the complete opposite experience. ***If you compare Albania to other European countries, I would put Albania as one of the top safest.***

I have been in Albania for the high season and the low season when I am nearly the only tourist in Saranda. Sure, I get weird looks like, "**what the hell are you still doing here?**", but despite the lack of other tourists, I feel completely comfortable and safe always.

Pickpocketing is practically non-existent and so are other petty crimes against tourists. That doesn't mean you shouldn't still be careful though. Albanians will always make you feel welcome and safe. So, in terms of understanding tourist safety, Albania is way ahead compared to a lot of other countries I have experienced.

Albanians also have a powerful sense of honesty and are incredibly welcoming people. They will offer you food and drinks on arrival and any help you need they will always be willing. They will treat you as part of their family.

The only argument I have had with Albanians is when I try to pay for my coffee but they will never let me!

Is Albania SAFE?

For a modern-day traveller, often people rely on the internet to gather information about their next visit. The internet is saturated with guides but when it comes to Albania there is hardly any information, which is one reason, in my opinion, people get nervous about coming here because they have no idea what to expect.

That, my friend, is the charm of Albania. You never really know what to expect. If you're not a relaxed person when it comes to travel then it may be a little difficult for you, but you will end up loving it, I'm sure.

I have travelled as a solo female through Albania and can confirm it's totally safe to do so. Most people are curious about the reason why I choose to live here, it is totally harmless.

Do not be fooled by misconceptions from people who have never travelled to Albania.

If you speak with a traveller that has been and experienced Albania, I'm sure you will get the same response as what I have just said. Of course, there are bad people in Albania, but there are also bad people everywhere around the world.

TRAVEL INSURANCE

When I travel, I use two either one of these travel insurance companies - *World Nomads or Safety Wing*. More about them below!

Safety Wing

Pro's of Safety Wing

- More affordable than World Nomads. You can get plans for as low as $42 for 4 weeks! It's a 1/3rd of the price of its major competitor.
- Full health coverage
- Very reliable company with better reviews than World Nomads on the likes of Trust Pilot.
- Worldwide coverage **INCLUDING** home coverage (up to 30 days every 3 months)
- 1 child between the age of 14 days – 10 years old can be included in your plan at NO extra cost

Con's of Safety Wing

- Coverage does NOT include Iran, North Korea or Cuba.
- Does NOT include electronics
- The policy does NOT include missed flights
- You are NOT covered for any pre-existing medical conditions

World Nomads

Pro's of World Nomads

- Full coverage from health (including dental visits) and travel delays (delayed, missed and cancelled flights)
- Option to insure expensive products like laptops, camera etc
- Worldwide coverage
- 2 options for plans (standard and explorer plan)

Con's of World Nomads

- More expensive than SafetyWing
- You are NOT covered for any pre-existing medical conditions that you had up to 6 months prior to purchasing the plan.
- Coverage does NOT cover Iran and North Korea

WHEN TO VISIT

When travellers come to Albania, they usually come here in the heat of summer, and while some LOVE it, many go away thinking it's just too hot! I want to show and inform you that Albania is not ONLY good for summer fun and tanning on the beach, in fact, but it might also be my personal least favourite time of year here in terms of the Albania weather. But it's actually a beautiful place all year-round.

I recommend travellers come in every season. There really is a reason to visit and enjoy the incredible Albanian weather all year round. Albania is a very diverse country.

There are a lot of spectacular places to visit. From historic and UNESCO towns like Gjirokastër and Berat to beautiful coastal cities like Saranda and Vlora. Then you have the north of Albania which hold incredible scenery such as the Albanian Alps and beautiful mountain towns like Kruja, the historical city of Albania.

Let me tell you more about Albanian weather.

ALBANIA WEATHER – WHAT IS IT LIKE?

The average low temperature in Albania during winter is around 1 degree.

In the south where I live (Saranda), it's always 1-4 degrees warmer than in northern cities like Shkoder. We get less rain and more sunny days.

In my opinion, Albania is one of the few countries in Europe that doesn't have an overbearing winter if you compare it to the likes of the UK, Poland, and Romania. The climate in Albania makes it a great winter destination for those who want to escape the bone-chilling cold like in other countries within Europe.

On average in the north they get over 290 days of sunshine and in the south they get over 325 days of sunshine!

Albania's weather is some of the best you can find in Europe. This is why I think the best time to visit Albania is any time!

SPRING

MARCH 20TH - JUNE 21ST

If you want to come and experience the optimal Albania weather, I highly recommend you come in Spring. This is my favourite season here and in my opinion, March is the best time to visit Albania! It's starting to get warm, the flowers are blossoming and there are virtually no tourists.

I really love the month of March, because this is the time you will literally have UNESCO sites to yourself. Since the temperature in Albania during March is also relatively cool, it's just pleasant to walk around outside or go hiking.

As you get closer to May, travellers start to visit Albania and then by summer European tourists are flocking (although it's nothing compared to Greece and Croatia yet!).

For many, this might seem like the perfect time to take advantage of the hot Albanian climate. But if you plan on venturing away from all the Albanian beaches, you'll find the Albania temperatures of summer overbearing.

Come to Albania in spring if you:

- Like travelling without tourists everywhere
- Like cheap prices (prices go up in summer)
- Don't mind wearing a jumper at night as the Albanian night temperatures are still chilly
- Like colourful destinations as beautiful flowers start to bloom and the country lights up!

SUMMER

21ST JUNE – SEPTEMBER 23RD

Summer is when Albania comes alive for tourists. Most people think this is when to visit Albania, and in fact, this is when 90% of people come to the country.

All the clubs, restaurants, and accommodation begin to open their doors as many close only to open for this season. It's a shame because as I said, spring and autumn are also magical.

This is when the south of Albania shines and you will find places like Ksamil (named the gem of the Albanian Riviera) absolutely packed with people.

The weather in Albania during summer can be intense! While the winter temperatures might be mild, the summer climate in Albania is anything but!

So, in terms of discovering Albania, summer is my least favourite. Also, because of the demand for tourists' prices rise, sometimes double. This happens in accommodation but also in restaurants and bars too.

Come to Albania in summer if you:

- Like the heat of the summer because in Saranda the temperatures hit 40 degrees!
- Like to party as beach bars and clubs are fully open along the Albanian Riviera
- Don't mind sharing the places you want to see with hordes of tourists (including cruise ship tourists in the likes of Saranda).

AUTUMN

SEPTEMBER 23RD – DECEMBER 21ST

Autumn is another favourite for me as the crowds go from the Albanian Riviera and it starts to become quiet again. Nature is beautiful, everything is tainted with orange colour in celebration of autumn and the weather doesn't really start to get cold until November.

Inland and northern regions it starts to get chilly a little earlier but from my experience, the heat of summer extends until early November.

This means that for those who want to experience the best Albanian weather but can't travel in Spring, autumn will also hit that sweet spot. And unlike winter, many seasonal places will still be open until September and October, but you'll have them to yourself.

Come to Albania in autumn if you:

- You like exploring places with fewer tourists
- Love cheaper prices, as businesses start to cut prices in half and some shut down for this season (in the Riviera)
- Like hiking as this is a great time for with the weather in Albania much cooler than in summertime with a lot fewer people
- Interested in exploring beautiful beaches with NO ONE in sight. Autumn and spring are my favourite time to explore the Albanian Riviera!

WINTER

DECEMBER 21ST - MARCH 20TH

An absolutely hidden magical time to visit the country. There's snow throughout which makes a great time for winter sports enthusiasts!

You will find the capital, Tirana filled with Christmas lights. You will find tourist spots absolutely empty which are great for really immersing yourself in the local culture.

Although it's cold, the climate in Albania makes for one of the mildest winters throughout Europe as the country is neighbours with Greece and we all know about Greek weather.

You will find along the Albanian Riveria that nearly all businesses are closed so just beware of that. I hope in the future that the tourists can spread throughout the season making a demand for businesses to stay open!

Come to Albania in winter if you:

- Like skiing and snowboarding at a fraction of the price. Places like Bigell in Dardha, Voskopoja, and Boga are good ones to try and accommodation is very affordable *(around 40-60 euros a night in ski resorts!)*
- Want to explore the capital of Tirana. A lot of locals come to Tirana after the summer season ends to work, so you will find a majority of the population here. It's a great time to soak up all the city has to offer!

Holidays & celebrations

NEW YEARS

New Years is the biggest holiday in Albania. This tradition came from communism as all religion was outlawed and the only holiday that isn't religious is New Years.

So, because of that, Albanians only could celebrate one holiday a year. The tradition has carried onto this day.

LIBERATION DAY

The day after Independence Day Albanians also celebrate liberation day.

This day celebrates when the country was liberated from Nazi Germany during World War 2.

SUMMER DAY

This is the biggest pagan holiday and an important holiday for Albanians and throughout the Balkans.

It celebrates the first day of the Albanian ancient calendar as well as the end of winter and the start of summer and rejuvenation of nature. If you want to celebrate this day then head to Elbasan. Here is the centre of celebrations with concerts and festivities for the day. People also make and eat ballakume – a sweet cookie.

You will notice people wearing a 2-string red and white bracelet named 'verore' which many start to wear March 1st.

After dita e vere is over they then tie the bracelet to a tree for good luck.

INDEPENDANCE DAY

This is the day that Albania declared its independence from The Ottoman Empire. It was proclaimed in Vlore in 1912.

Only 6 days later the first government of Albania was created and led by Ismail Qemali.

A prominent moment was when Ismail waved the first flag of independent Albania from the balcony of the assembly of Vlora.

This flag was inspired by Skanderbeg's (a national hero) flag which had been used 400 years beforehand.

PRICES IN ALBANIA

Albania is an incredibly affordable destination. This is the reason why many choose Albania as their holiday destination.

You can grab a beer for about €1-2 and a meal between €3-5. A hostel bed with breakfast and a beer can cost as low as €7 and a hotel room for around €30.

There are many great options for all budgets, whether you're a backpacker or prefer a more luxury holiday.

Is Albania cheap to live as a foreigner? Yes. Albania living costs are so low compared to the rest of Europe, you will be able to live much nicer for much less.

But please keep in mind that this is coming from my perspective as a foreigner who is not earning a local wage here in Albania. These are considered high for Albania prices as the wage for locals is very low. The average salary in Albania is around €150-400 per month if they are in a job that's considered average (like a waiter), so the prices in Albania are considered high.

EXAMPLES OF PRICES

FOOD & DRINK

- Expresso: 50-100lek
- Cocktail: 600-1000lek
- Coca cola: 150lek
- Beer: 150lek
- Wine (1L): 600lek
- Greek salad: 400lek
- Mussels: 600lek
- Pizza: 500-1000lek
- Fried calamari: 1200lek
- Souvlaki: 200lek
- Fish/chicken soup: 350-450 lek

ACTIVITES

- Monthly gym membership 3000lek
- Fitness class: 300-500lek
- Movie ticket: 600lek
- Day Boat trip in Saranda: €30-40

ACCOMMODATION

- Hostel bed: 700 - 1300lek per night
- Guesthouse room: 2500 - 4000lek +
- Hotel room Luxury: 7000-13000lek+

These prices can change quite a lot depending on season and location. Saranda for example is the most expensive city in Albania so during the summer prices are high.

Prices in the north of Albania are much lower.

MISCELLANEOUS

- Unlimited Wifi: 2000lek
- Monthly power bill: 2500-6000lek
- Rent for 1bd house: €150-400
- Bus ticket from Saranda to Tirana: 1300lek

TRAVELLING AROUND ALBANIA

Travelling in Albania is something you may have never expected. Many expect Albania to be dangerous, not friendly and ugly, but tourists are surprised when they visit and learn that none of those is true.

Albania is safe for tourists. The Albanians are some of the friendliest and most welcoming in the world. They will treat you like one of their own.

Albania is far from ugly. The beaches, mountains and people confirm that. Albania tourism is thriving!

When you travel to Albania, you shouldn't plan too far ahead. Everything is flexible, from bus timetables to itineraries.

I would suggest having a rough plan but the option to be a little flexible with it.

When travelling to Albania, you will have to learn to trust the transport system. There are timetables but quite often they are wrong or have been changed. There's only one train ride you can take, so it's all about furgons, buses and hitchhiking!

FURGONS

This is the most popular way to get around Albania. Furgons are essentially minibuses that are privately owned and not licensed.

Sometimes they have a timetable, sometimes they don't. They will usually travel to smaller villages and also more popular routes like from Saranda to Gijrokastër and Berat.

The furgon is usually crammed with a lot of people so, in the high season, it can be a little cramped, but this is usually my preferred transport choice. They will drop you off at any point along the way, you just have to let them know.

Furgons are definitely more intimate than big coaches!

The good thing about furgons is you can flag one down and they will usually stop for you and let you on if it's not full.

So, if hitchhiking fails then you always have that as a backup option as long as you're not in the middle of nowhere.

In terms of the timetables there are some but most of the time they change. The best option is to ask a local as they always seem to know everything about transport.

Most likely the bus driver will probably be a relation or friend, I'm not kidding. Everyone knows everyone.

BUSES

Buses run for more popular and longer routes like for example from Saranda to Tirana. They also have rough timetables. Be prepared to share the bus with car motors, washing machines, and other household essentials.

Usually, the buses act as a delivery service as well. You can do the same as with the furgons and tell the driver where you want to get off, they will usually stop. Buses will sometimes stop for hitchhikers too if they aren't full.

For longer trips that are over 3 hours, you will stop halfway for a toilet and food break for 15-30minutes.

Tickets

For the longer bus rides, you will usually need a ticket beforehand, especially if it's high season. In low season you can just buy it on the day.

For the furgons sometimes you will buy a ticket from the driver or just give him cash when you arrive at the destination.

Top tips

- Be prepared for the driver to smoke. It's not uncommon for the driver to be a chain smoker.
- Bring snacks and water with you
- Always carry cash
- Be flexible as sometimes the bus just won't show up. If you're relying on a flight, I would recommend getting to Tirana earlier than needed just in case.

BUS + FURGON STATIONS

In each city, there's either a bus station or a bus road/s. Albania's bus stations are a lot less official than you think and most of the time it's just a car park with a whole lot of buses.

Tirana

Tirana, there are two bus stations for Albania– one for buses going north and one for buses going south. They are about a 15-minute walk from each other so make sure you get the right one! The station for buses going south is the further one away from the city.

As soon as you turn up to either of these bus stations you will hear an array of men asking where you're going. Just scream which place you want to go and one of them will show you to the bus. They are not asking for a tip, they usually are the guys who help the driver fill the bus up with people.

Saranda

Saranda, the buses go from a few places, but they are all very near to each other. There is a couple of 'bus roads' in the middle of the city. Usually, the ones to and from Greece go from outside the ticket office, which is opposite the red building called Partizani.

The buses that go within Albania are found on the street Rruga Flamurit, near the ruins and the park. If you ask anyone there where you want to go, they will lead you to the right bus. The buses and furgons will have a sign in the window saying where they are going

Shkoder

Shkoder, there are two locations. One for buses going south to Tirana, which is located opposite the radio station.

The other one is on the opposite side of the big roundabout near the mosque. Again, just yell where you're going, and someone will take you to your bus.

Berat

Berat, the bus station is located just outside of the city. You will need to catch a bus, which is situated next to the petrol station (across the road from the bus station). Or you can catch a taxi (500lek) or hitchhike into Berat as it's about a 10-minute drive away.

Hitchhiking

Hitchhiking in Albania is incredibly popular with tourists and locals. It's very normal to hitchhike and you will never wait for more than 20 minutes (usually). In my experience, it's taken no longer than 5 minutes! There's no real art to hitchhiking. Stick your thumb out, make sure you're visible and that you're in a spot that's easy for someone to pull over.

Although in Albania they will stop in the middle of the street – that's Albanian driving for you!

Is it safe? Yes, as long as you listen to your instincts. If someone pulls over and you don't get a good feeling, then just wave them on and try again.

From all the travellers I have come across, most of them hitchhiked and none of them had any problems with it so that is saying something!

DRIVING IN ALBANIA

If you visit Albania it can be a great idea to hire a car in Albania. That way you will see more of the country and get to stop at all the great hidden spots most tourists would completely miss.

When it comes to driving in Albania, it should come with caution as signs and road laws seem to be merely suggestions for Albanians.

Speeding, weaving in and out of traffic, and overtaking on blind corners is very common. When driving in Albania always drive with caution and beware of all sides of the car as people can and will overtake you without your knowledge.

You **MUST** put your lights on when driving in Albania. There is a law that states it. Whether the law is followed through, that's another story. Better to leave them on than not.

Another thing that they are very tough on is always carrying your driver's license. Albanians can be put straight into jail if they don't have their license on them when an officer asks. This applies to foreigners too.

I have had friends who didn't have their licences on them and it was a horrible experience. There was a lot of shouting, taken 'hostage' in a police station and a huge hassle! **So please, always carry your licence.**

COMPANIES TO RENT FROM

There are several different companies you can try. Some recommendations are:

- EuroCar (They have an office in Tirana and Saranda and is one of the most popular companies for tourists)
- SurPrice
- Hertz Albania
- Drive Albania (4×4 for hire)

There are lots more companies that hire cars. Within Tirana airport, you can see many offices. In Saranda, the main companies are located near the port.

I have rented from 'Buy Home Albania' which is a Saranda office in the centre. It's a real estate company but they also hire cars and scooters for a very reasonable price.

PRICES OF RENTING

Obviously, prices vary from company to company and depending on which month you are renting it. You can rent a car for as low as €15 and as high as €100 per day. I would say the average would be between €15-40 per day.

It will also depend on whether you want a manual or automatic and what kind of car you would like. Automatic is more expensive.

BEWARE OF THE ERRATIC DRIVERS

There are a lot of people in Albania who don't go by the rules. There's a lot of excessive speeding, overtaking on blind corners and erratic driving.

There's nothing that you can do about it, just be aware when you're driving and what others are doing around you. Keep your distance from the cars in front of you and always make a note if the car in front of you has its brake lights working, a lot of the time they are broken.

ALWAYS CARRY CASH FOR PETROL

Most petrol stations do not have a card machine. You will usually pay cash to the person who will put the petrol in your car.

Just pull up, tell them how much Lek worth of petrol you want, wait and then pay the person directly.

PARKING

You may notice that a common thing Albanians do is not park properly. They will pull over, put their hazard lights on and run into a store, or go have coffee.

In cities around Albania, long-term parking can be hard to come by and you might find yourself driving for a while to find a car park.

DON'T TRUST GOOGLE MAPS

I have found on numerous road trips that what google maps say is different from reality. The best way to combat this is to use google satellite and see in real-time what the road looks like, or if it's even a road!

Another tip would be to ask the locals. The word for car is 'Makine' and the word for the road is 'Rruga'.

Put those two words together, point in the direction you want to go and see what happens!

DROPPING OFF YOUR CAR

In Albania, there are not plentiful offices of the same company. A company in Tirana will probably not have an office in Saranda or Shkoder where you want to drop it.

Always check with the car company first. Maybe they will let you but with a big fee. The only recommendation I have is the company 'EuroCar'.

VISITING NEIGHBOURING COUNTRIES

If you do want to visit one of Albania's neighbours, then always check with the company if this is allowed.

You will need to get extra car papers if you do wish to take it overseas.

REMEMBER

Before you leave for your road trip ALWAYS take many pictures and videos of the car to have evidence just in case, they accuse you of scratching or denting the car when you bring it back.

If there are any minor damages to the car when you get it, be sure to document that and talk with the car company and confirm that they see these damages before you hire it.

POLICE & BRIBES

Police may pick on international number plates or if they can see a foreigner driving. It's always best to stick to the rules. If you do get pulled over for something you didn't commit, always ask for evidence. Police can also give on the spot fines of up to 5000 Lek but that's if you do something wrong!

Bribery used to be obvious but now they don't try with foreigners so much as the penalty for them getting caught doing this is high.

LAST TIPS

- Tirana centre traffic is always bad and an absolute headache. If you can avoid driving within Tirana, then do it!
- Hitchhiking is very common in Albania with foreigners and locals
- If you are coming to Albania in the winter be aware of the weather. Flash-flooding and ice on the road can happen in an instant and can be very dangerous.

ROAD RULES TO KNOW

01 **Always carry your licence:** Make sure you always have your licence on you. For Albanians, there are harsh penalties for not carrying your license. Being a foreigner, you are in an even more vulnerable position so don't risk it!

02 **Drive on the right side of the road:** In Albania make sure you always stick to the right-hand side of the road!

03 **Give way to the left.** You should always give way at intersections to the person on your left. The person entering a roundabout has to give way but you should be aware that many locals believe it's the other way around from an old rule.

04 **Keep your lights on:** When driving in Albania make sure you have your headlights on, all the time, at every part of the day.

05 **Keep to the speed limits:** For no reason, the speed might change to as low as 30 Km for absolutely no reason in the middle of nowhere. Police will look for any excuse to pull you over so always keep to it, no matter how ridiculous.

06 **Keep off your cell phone:** It's illegal to drive whilst using a cell phone in Albania.

07 **Wait for the Police:** If you are in an accident you are obliged to wait for the police, even if it's small. If you don't, then the insurance for your car will be invalid as they need a police report.

ALBANIA TRAVEL TIPS

GO WITH THE FLOW

This is the biggest Albania travel tip because if there's something you should know about Albania, it's to relax and go with the flow! Albania is unlike other countries you might have visited. Don't expect a bus to be on time, don't expect everything to go your way, don't expect anything. It's good to have no expectations with Albania, that way you will experience the real Albania.

Albanians are very relaxed. Everything takes time, appointments are merely suggestions most of the time. If someone says to you 'I'll have it done by tomorrow' they probably mean they will have it done for you next month.

GO TO THE ALBANIAN RIVIERA

You cannot go to Albania and only visit Tirana, you are missing out. The Albanian Riviera is home to some of the most beautiful beaches I have seen. You will find many hidden coves, beaches and quaint villages.

My favourite little village is upper Qeparo, it's a half-abandoned village which sits on a mountain and overlooks the sea.

GET USED TO THE STARING

The staring is something you will have to get used to if it's not common for your culture. I have lived here since 2017 and it's still something I struggle with.

Staring is part of Albanian culture. They love to people watch, it might just be the favourite Albanian pastime. Don't be offended if someone is staring at you, it's normal!

SAY YES

One of my favourite parts about Albania is the hospitality. They have world-class hospitality. It doesn't matter who you are, where you come from, what you do - you will be welcomed with open arms. Saying yes should be an important Albania travel tip because during your time in Albania you will probably be asked many times if you want something to eat, drink, go and see something etc.

Albanians love being hospitable and, I have learned that no means nothing. For example, when I visit my boyfriend's family if his mother asks if I want chocolate, I MUST eat that chocolate - there's no other way around it.

EAT THE LOCAL FOOD

This is a great tip for tourists because many people come here expecting the finest salmon or great sushi. The reality is you're going to be disappointed. Don't expect western food, instead try the local cuisine. Eat what comes in abundance here in Albania! For example, along the Albanian Riviera make sure you try seafood. It's fresh, delicious and (most of the time) comes straight from the sea onto your dinner plate.

You can find some good western-style restaurants in Tirana, but it's not going to be as good as you can probably get while your home. Instead, dive deep into Albanian food – it's fresh, delicious and healthy!

TALK POLITICS

When you come to Albania you will soon notice that Albanians LOVE to talk politics. Unfortunately, there are still a lot of problems in the country that still are yet to be solved.

No jobs, wages are low and the quality of living in low. Albania is hard to live in and hard to get ahead as an Albanian. You will certainly have these kinds of talks with Albanians when you come here

LEARN A FEW WORDS

Albanians really appreciate you trying to speak their language, even if you do get it wrong! The Albanian language is unlike any other language in the world – that's a fact, not an opinion. There is no other European language that is like Albanian.

The Albanian language has its own roots!

Fun fact: The North and the south have different dialects so they cannot understand what each other are saying usually.

LEARN THE HISTORY

Albania has had an interesting but difficult past. To understand the country and the people you should learn a little about the recent history. From the 1940s until the 1990's Albania was under communist rule which meant there were strict restrictions. Some compare it with North Korea.

After communism fell, 2/3 of Albania's population lost all of their life savings due to a pyramid scheme. When the scheme collapsed, rioting begun, the government collapsed and that was the start of a civil war that lasted for around 6-7 months.

KNOW THE PRICES

Unfortunately, like nearly every place in the world, there are going to be people who try and rip you off because you're a tourist. The best thing you can do is to do some research and get to know the prices.

In the last year, I have noticed it more in Albania. I think it's due to tourism rising and more people seeing the opportunity to completely rip tourists off and making them pay triple for something.

For example, a taxi from the airport to Tirana should cost around 2000 lek. I had a taxi driver try and charge me 5000 lek for it. A great tip is to ask the locals how much certain things should cost if you get talking to them.

TALK PHILOSOPHY

On top of politics, Albanians also love to talk about philosophy. This is something I noticed within the first year of living here. You will get into deep conversations about existence, language, the mind and why are we here?!

TRY THE PIZZA

Albanians make incredible pizza! Italy is only just across the water so it's a given that they have a little bit of Italian influence. Also, a lot of Albanians moved to Italy and found work in pizza restaurants and have learned the art of Italian pizza.

Now they have brought that back to Albania and you can find quality pizza. I'm sorry Italians, but I have had better pizza in Albania than I have had in Italy.

TAKE CASH

Albania is a cash society. You won't find many shops or restaurants taking Eftpos, although that is slowly changing.

When you come to Albania you should try to go to an atm as soon as you can get some LEK out. Most businesses also take euros. Some ATMs charge a fee for cash.

I have been charged as much as 800lek to get money out. Some have a 500lek fee and some are free! You can also get euro cash out of at least one atm but best to ask a local where that is.

DON'T UNDERESTIMATE THE RAKI

Raki is the local moonshine and it's strong, very strong. In fact, raki can be upwards of 70% proof and the great thing, you never really know how strong it is until it hits you. But raki is not made for getting drunk. It goes deeper than that.

You will see old men having a glass of raki with their morning coffee. Albanians believe raki is good for the heart, good for the bones, good for everything - but in moderation of course.

Raki is also used in hospitals and as medicine for toothaches and wounds.

It's the perfect all-round drink! Most families who live in a village will make their own raki, and a lot of it so it lasts them a while.

If you visit Tirana, make sure you visit a bar called Komiteti. It's a raki bar with dozens of flavours!

DON'T LISTEN TO THE MISCONCEPTIONS

Unfortunately, Albania has many misconceptions. Mostly due to misinformation, no information and the movie Taken. Actually, only one of the actors who plays an Albanian is actually Albanian.

They are constantly portrayed as bad guys, drug dealers, drug lords, gangs etc. Although Albania has a history of some of those things, doesn't nearly every country in the world? Albania is completely safe, in fact, I have felt safer here than in western European countries

The crime rate is extremely low against tourists, in fact non-existent.

And the mafia? Well, let's just say there's more money to be made elsewhere. You don't have to ever worry about that sort of thing. Albanians are incredibly friendly, very helpful and vow to always keep you safe while visiting or living in their country.

If I ever have a situation or need help, there's always a bunch of people offering to help, even if they can't, they will find someone!

28 PLACES TO VISIT

28 PLACES TO VISIT

21
HIMARE
22
FINIQ
23
PERMET
BORSH
24
28
PLACES
TO VISIT
25
SARANDA
BUTRINT
26
27
KSAMIL
28
GJIROKASTRA

TIRANA

THINGS TO DO

The cool city of Tirana is one to watch closely as it's becoming increasingly popular with travellers around the world. The capital city of Albania has a lot of history, the coolest bars and great food at an affordable price.

It is a great city to spend a few days in and get a grip on the hub and beating heart of Albania.

WANDER AROUND SKANDERBEG SQUARE

The national hero, George Castoit who stopped the Ottoman Empire from entering further into central Europe. The square is a nice place to people watch and chill out when the sun is shining. Near here you will find the National Museum, Clock Tower and Et'hem Bey Mosque.

This is one of the great things to do in Tirana at night too when everyone has finished work and all catching up with each other. At Christmas time you will find beautiful markets here too!

MARVEL AT THE NATIONAL MUSEUM

The national museum is the largest museum in Albania. It's a great place to learn more about Albania's past. You must admire the impressive mosaic at the front of the building representing Albanians marching from ancient Illyria times to World War 2.

ADMIRE THE CLOCK TOWER

This tower was built in the 1820's and still stands strong today. From Mon to Fri (9 am - 4 pm), Sat (9 am - 2 pm). It's worth the climb to get a great view of the square.

LOOK AT ET'HEM BEY MOSQUE

This 18th-century mosque was closed during the communist regime but opened back up in 1991. The interior design and architecture are stunning and worth a look inside to marvel at the detail of the facades.

HOUSE OF LEAVES

The House of Leaves is the one of the best museums in the city. Here you can get an insight into the national intelligence service, and the chilling history from when it was occupied by Germans in World War 2.

After the war, it was then regained by the Albanian government to spy on Albanians during the communist times and convict them of political crimes.

THINGS TO DO

VISIT GRAND PARK

This is a popular nature chill-out spot for the locals. Admire the artificial lake on a sunny and bright day or join the locals on a daily run or walk around the park. It's a nice place to hang out to get away from the hustle and bustle of the busy city.

VISIT BUNK ART 2

Bunk Art 2 is the former anti-nuclear bunker for internal affairs. This is located right in the city, near Skanderbeg square. There are 24 rooms, a great hall and an apartment for the former minister of internal affairs. If you're wondering what to see in Tirana first, I highly recommend coming here!

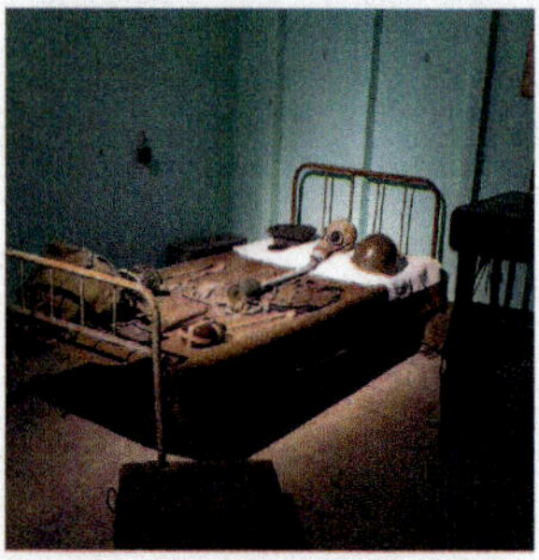

VISIT BUNK ART

Bunk Art is an exhibition located on the outskirts of Tirana dedicated to the history of the communist army and what happened to Albanians during that time. You will get to see Enver Hoxha's luxury bunker and many other interesting exhibitions here.

TAKE A FREE WALKING TOUR

What better way to start your day in Tirana by doing a free walking tour. Every day at 10 am or 6pm you can meet the guide outside the Opera House for a free 2-hour tour around the city. This is one of the top things to do in Tirana when you first arrive so you can get your bearings of the city.

POSTBLLOKU (OPEN AIR MUSEUM)

Although it may be not as impressive as you would expect an outdoor museum to be I think it is worth a look.

In this small park, you will find a fragment of the Berlin Wall, a bunker and remains from an Albanian labour camp during the communist regime.

During the communist era, tens of thousands were imprisoned for 'political crimes' and sent to labour camps. Spaç Prison was a labour camp where many lost their lives. It is often referred to as the Albanian Auschwitz.

THINGS TO DO

TAKE THE CABLE CAR UP MOUNT DAJTI

This mountain towers 1613meters high and 1000 meters of that can be reached via cable car. From the mountain, you can get a great view over the city. Note that the cable car is closed on Tuesdays.

VISIT THE DISTRICT OF BLLOKU

This district used to be home to rich and famous leaders of the communist regimes. Nowadays it has been transformed into a trendy, hip district of Tirana. There are plenty of good restaurants and bars to check out here.

VISIT ENVER HOXHA'S HOUSE

Although not open to the public, you can see the former communist leaders Enver Hoxha's old house from outside the gates. There are plans to open this as a sort of museum to the public in the future.

LOOK AT THE NEW MARKET OF TIRANA

This Tirana market is a great addition to the city. Here you will find cafes galore, market treats and the like. You can find some great homemade products and handicrafts situated here!

VISIT THE PYRAMID

This communism monument was built as a museum dedicated to the old communist leader, Enver Hoxha. There is only an Albanian broadcast company operating out of there. Its crumbling façade is popular with graffiti artists and young people climbing and chilling out around what is now known as 'The Pyramid'. *They are currently renovating this pyramid!*

WATCH THE SUNSET FROM SKYBAR

If you are looking for an epic spot for sunset then head to the Skybar for a drink. You get a great panoramic view of the city.

THINGS TO DO

TANNER BRIDGE

This Ottoman-style bridge gives you a look into what the city used to look like. It dates back to the 18th century. You can find the bridge near the Tanner Mosque.

This bridge was mostly used to bring livestock and produce into the city from Deber.

CHECK THE MARKETS

I have to say, Tirana has some of the best second-hand markets I have ever been to! For the best ones, it's a good idea to ask the locals where they suggest going. There are quite a few scattered around the city, one of the best is near the old train station

TAKE A COOKING CLASS

Want to learn more about Albanian food and how to make it? Take a cooking class to learn more in-depth about Albanian food.

The tour starts at 1 pm and you will learn all about how to make some Albania's best dishes!

WHERE TO EAT

SALT Tirana: This is one of the best restaurants in Tirana serving a Meditteranean style menu with seafood, sushi, tacos and more.

Oda: Here you can find traditional Albanian food in a traditional setting. You will find quality food, friendly staff and beautiful decor! Oda is one of the best places to eat. If you want to visit Tirana but are not sure what to do, going for a traditional meal can be a great start to learning more about the culture through its food!

The Tea Room: If you want to try some of the best homemade cakes and sweets then head here. It's right on the river and is a nice cosy little café to try!

Birrari Ke Tori: If you're looking for a good hearty meal then pick this one. It's a great BBQ house with fantastic meat plates and chicken wings at an affordable price.

Duff Bar: If you're craving some American food in Tirana like burgers and other greasy treats, then I can recommend checking out Duff Bar. I go here whenever I need a fix of the fattiest food possible and it never disappoints. They have the best burger in Tirana!

Stephens Centre: Also, another recommendation for American-like food. They do a great eggs benedict and good coffee here. It's right next to New Market.

TIRANA

NIGHTLIFE

Kometiti: My favourite bar in all of Tirana is Kometiti! They have oodles of different flavoured raki. The bar is set in a type of museum-style with lots of historic knick-knacks to marvel at.

Radio bar: If you're looking for a great cocktail bar then Radio Bar is the one! It's worth a visit just to admire the eclectic interior design of this place.

Hemingway Bar: This is another good bar in Tirana that deserves a visit whilst you're here. They have a large selection of cocktails and other treats for you to try. You will find the atmosphere of this place fantastic!

Folie Terrace: During the summer this place is packed out. If you're looking to pull an all-nighter, then head here. Note that it is only open during the summer months.

Arena Nightclub: This modern club is a popular one and another great option if you're wanting to party all night! This is one of the best nightclubs in Tirana.

Lollipop: This is probably the most famous nightclub in the city. It's known for its EDM and can hold hundreds of people.

WHERE TO STAY IN TIRANA

Trip'n Hostel: If you're looking for a good hostel to stay in there is no other option than Trip'n Hostel! I absolutely loved my stay here. The owners are super lovely. If you're looking for a fun and chilled hostel then make sure you choose this one, trust me, you won't be disappointed! The breakfast here is amazing, and they have their own bar where they also make their own beer.

Hotel Colosseo: This is one of the top hotels in Tirana. Comes with a great free breakfast and is right in the city centre.

The Plaza Hotel Tirana: This Tirana luxury hotel (5 stars) is not to be missed on your trip to Tirana. It's got everything you would ever need including spa, gym, breakfast and 3 restaurants on-site.

BERAT

THINGS TO DO

A visit to the beautiful UNESCO town of Berat is not to be missed on your adventures through Albania. It is one of my favourite towns in the country. Berat seems to have a charm like no other place, and there are so many amazing things to do in Berat to make you instantly fall in love with it.

It's famously known for its white Ottoman-style houses which also gave Berat another name – the town of one thousand windows. It's a small place but you could easily spend more than a few days enjoying the numerous Berat attractions, soaking up the culture and visiting other sites nearby.

The town itself is over 2400 years old and holds an important part of Albanian history. It's one of the only places in the world where residents still live within castle walls.

VISIT THE BERAT CASTLE

You simply cannot visit Berat without taking a walk (or drive) to the castle which overlooks the city. Berat Castle dates all the way back to the 4th century, although most of the current remains are from the 13th century. The castle even still has examples of both Ottoman and Byzantine architecture within its walls.

Inside Berat Castle, you will see old houses where people still live today. You can also explore the old churches and mosques on site. Berat Castle is special because it allows you to see a glimpse of Albanian history. The castle also gives an almost 360-degree view of the surrounding landscape.

GAZE AT THE HOLY TRINITY CHURCH

There are ten remaining churches at Berat Castle, but none as impressive as the Holy Trinity Church. This church dates to the 13th century and has the most beautiful frescoes inside. While you're at the castle make sure you take time to look at the church.

Even if you're not interested in the history, it's one of the best Berat attractions for a view over the town, and maybe the most stunning views a church has ever had!

THINGS TO DO

MARVEL AT THE OLD TOWN

With old Ottoman houses and a unique charm, it's a must to wander through the old cobbled streets of Berat and take in the culture.

One of the best things to do in Berat is to just sit at a local cafe and watch the locals go by. A good dose of people watching is a must-do!

TAKE A WINE TOUR

Easily one of the most popular things to do in Berat is taking a wine tour, and that's because the town is home to three wineries:

- **Cabo Winery**

I highly recommend visiting Cabo. It's located just outside of the city. They do wine tours of the winery and the grapes. You can also decide to do a tasting. You will taste several wines along with a food platter for a very good price. Their wine is some of the best in Albania!

- **Nurellari Winery**

Another fine winery is Nurellari. It's not as popular as Cabo but it's still very delicious, they have superb red wine here. This winery used to be a storage facility for food during communism. You can book a wine tour with them to learn more about their wine and history.

- **Luani Winery**

The third winery is Luani which started in 1960 as a state-owned winery but has been a privately-owned winery for the last 25 years. They have a lot of variety at Luani so make sure you stop over to taste and hear more about the establishment!

MOUNT TOMORR

Like Bogova Waterfall, this is one of the best things to do near Berat, and why it's worth staying a few days. If you love hiking, then a visit to Mount Tomorr should be on your list.

Not only is mount Tomorr a beautiful place for an adventure, but it plays an important part in Albanian mythology and folklore. It's also a place for religious worshippers, there is a festival at the end of august where pilgrims gather from the Bektashi sect to celebrate.

THINGS TO DO

VISIT BOGOVA WATERFALL

If you have more than a few days in Berat, things to do might seem limited. However, about a 50-minute drive away is one of the best natural attractions near Berat – Bogova waterfall. You can opt to do a tour here or take a bus to the nearby village of Bogova then walk for 30 minutes until you reach the waterfall.

If you're visiting by car you can park in the (sort of) carpark then walk for around 5-10 minutes until you reach it. The water is cold all year round so it makes for a great option in those hot summer months!

VISIT THE ETHNOGRAPHIC MUSEUM

To learn more about the town's history, one of the first things you'll want to do when you visit Berat is head to the ethnographic museum.

While there may not be as many things to do in Berat as bigger cities like Tirana, this fascinating museum is still one of the top Berat attractions for a reason! Plus, it's a great way to avoid the hot summer sun!

Originally a house, the building has been turned into a museum where you can see how a traditional Berat house is set up from furniture to household objects and even a well. The house's architecture is incredibly unique, as well.

WANDER GORICA AND SEE THE VIEW FROM THE BRIDGE

Gorica is a neighbourhood just over the bridge in Berat and where my favourite hostel (Berat backpackers) is located. It might not seem like one of the must see Berat attractions, but this little neighbourhood is old with cobble lined streets. To get a dose of daily life in

Berat take a walk through the old houses and see the view of the ottoman houses from across the bridge.

There is a great photo opportunity here to capture the town of one thousand windows!

BERAT

WHERE TO EAT

Here are some top recommendations for restaurants in Berat. Make sure you try some of the delicious traditional Albanian food while you're in Berat!

- Restaurant Mangalemi
- Homemade Food Lili
- Wildor
- Antigoni Restaurant
- Heavens kitchen

WHERE TO STAY IN BERAT

Traditional house: There is a 300-year-old guest house called Nonaj House which comes highly recommended if you would like a look into and stay in one of the oldest houses in Berat.

Hotel: Some of the most highly recommended hotels include Hotel Mangalemi, Guesthouse Arben Elezi and Hani i Xheblatit.

Hostel: There is only one hostel that I recommend you stay at when you visit and that's Berat backpackers. This is one of my favourite hostels in Albania. It's in one of the old Berat houses and is one of the most beautiful and fun hostels in Albania.

The breakfast is delicious, and they also offer different tours which you can join. In the summer you also have the option to camp in the backyard.

KORÇË

THINGS TO DO

Upon a recent trip to Korce, I was pleasantly surprised at how incredible it was, and confused as to why I hadn't visited sooner! The city is a popular weekend trip for Albanians who live in Tirana as it's about a 3-hour drive from city to city.

Korca is now being voted as one of the top places to visit in Albania but tourism is still relatively new to international travellers.

The city is filled with great things to do from exploring the market, getting the best view of the city and eating your heart out on Qofte, which is Albanian meatballs!

GET THE BEST VIEW OF THE CITY

One of the best things to do in Korca is to climb the stairs of the red tower. Here you get an amazing view of the city. Entry only costs 50 Lek. I highly recommend visiting at sunset when you can enjoy the view of the city at golden hour.

Take note that the elevator doesn't work to take you to the top so you do have to walk around 8 flights of stairs.

HANG OUT IN PAZARI I VJETËR

This is my favourite part about Korce, the bazaar! This is the most popular place to hang out and wander. The cobbled lined streets, old architecture and ambience mimic something from a fairytale.

The Old bazaar was renovated recently and has really given it a new lease on life. There are many bars, restaurants and boutique to check out. Don't forget to pick up Albanian souvenir while you are there.

THINGS TO DO

GAZE AT THE LARGEST ORTHODOX CHURCH IN ALBANIA

This beautiful church is probably the most impressive one I have ever seen. The architecture is just incredible. This is actually the largest Orthodox church within Albania.

It was built in 1995 after the original cathedral was destroyed during communism as all religion was banned throughout the country.

EAT QOFTE

Qofte is one of the best things to eat in Albania and throughout the Balkans (except for vegetarians or vegans!).

Qofte is mince with spices, onion and some other secret ingredients. It's like meatballs but with way more flavour.

The outside should be a little crispy with the inside being soft and sort of melting in your mouth. I'm drooling while writing this if you can't tell already.

One of the best places I had Qofte (said chofta) was in a restaurant within the old bazaar.

HAVE KORCA IN KORCA

While you're a beer-drinking then you will notice on your time in Albania that you may have the beer called Korca, well that's because it's produced in Korce.

There is a brewery in Korca which is popular. I also suggest going to a bar within the old bazaar and enjoying a cold glass of Korca while people watching.

VISIT THE MUSEUM OF MEDIEVAL ART

Korce have many great museums but one of the most interesting is the museum of medieval art! This museum has over 7000 pieces of art and was started in 1980.

THINGS TO DO

TAKE A NIGHTLY GJIRO (WALK) DOWN SHËN GJERGJ

This is the main boulevard of Korca and is a great place to soak in local life. Here you will find many cafes and bars to have a coffee or a nightcap in and it's a great spot to people watch.

At one end you have the cathedral and on the other, you have the red tower.

VISIT THE NATIONAL EDUCATION MUSEUM

If you want to learn more about the Albania culture and language then this is a great place to do so! This building was the first school in Albania which opened in 1887.

This museum will show you the struggles of the Albanian language which is so complex and not similar to any other language in the world!

TAKE A DAY TRIP TO VOSKOPOJË

I had never heard of Voskopojë until my Albanian partner mentioned it.

Voskopojë is a popular place for Albanian tourists but I didn't see many international tourists while I was there. It's such a beautiful place which is known for having an abundant amount of churches.

In fact, originally this small sweet village had 24 churches all built between the 16th and 18th centuries. Only 8 of them stand today, which is still a lot for such a small place!

Voskopojë is only a 30-minute drive from Korca, making it a fantastic day trip to the countryside

KORCE

WHERE TO EAT

If you want a great bite to eat then make sure you try these restaurants below as they are quality food and local prices.

Taverna Vasili is a small taverna serving delicious Albanian food that won't break the bank.

Vila Cofiel is one of the best restaurants in Korce. If you want to be introduced to the Albanian food scene you simply must come here. If you do visit make sure you try the kërnacka which is meatballs - they are simply delicious!

Café-Museum Komiteti is the perfect place for a nightcap. Make sure you try the raki!

WHERE TO STAY IN KORCE

One of the most recommended places to stay in Korce is **Villa Ester**. It's one of the most beautiful accommodation options with the best reviews!

Hani i Pazarit boutique hotel is a popular pick for many travellers coming to Korca because of its history. It's located in the old bazaar which means it's the perfect place to explore nearby sites. It's also set in a 350-year-old building and they have done a great job at preserving the history of Albania.

I would highly recommend booking in advance if you do come to Korca, especially at the weekends. Things can get booked up very quickly as Korca is one of the main destinations for Albanians.

POGRADEC

THINGS TO DO

Pogradec is located on the opposite side of Ohrid Lake to Ohrid, Macedonia. This lake city is a relaxing getaway for anyone looking for a classic lake holiday. It's quiet and very peaceful here! Pogradec and the surrounding area is a UNESCO protected site.

The city is popular in the summer months due to the Meditteranean climate. It's nestled between the mountain ranges above and the lake down below making it a picturesque holiday getaway. Plus there are many great things to do nearby too making it a fantastic place to base yourself for adventures nearby.

POGRADEC BEACH

One of the best things to do year-round is checking out the lakefront and beach.

This can get super busy during the summer months with tourists and locals cooling off in Ohrid Lake. During the summer there are sun-beds you can rent for the day.

There is no beach like Pogradec beach in Lake Ohrid, making it one-of-a-kind!

EAT KORAN

Koran is a fish found in Lake Ohrid that is similar to Salmon.

You can find most restaurants in Pogradec serving this unique fish so make sure you give it a try whilst on your travels here.

THINGS TO DO

VISIT LIN

The sleepy town of Lin is a pretty unique stop within Albania. Although there isn't a lot to do here, Lin is a peaceful village, mostly inhabited by the older generation, that sits on Lake Ohrid. I highly recommend walking or driving to the hill which sits above Lin. There is an archaeology park as well as one of the best views of the area from here.

DRILONI NATIONAL PARK

Only a 5 minute drive from Drilioni Beach is a beautiful nature escape called Drilioni National Park. If you want to get away from the city hustle and bustle, take a trip here and take in the serenity of the park. You can rent rowboats for only 500lek and take in the views from the stream if you wish!

VISIT TUSHEMISHT

The nearby village of Tushemisht is one I had never heard of until my boyfriend pointed it out. Apparently this place is very famous with Albanians because of an actress who starred in one of the most popular shows in Albania. However, foreigner tourists here are rare so this is very much still an off the beaten path recommendation, The village is very unique because springs wrap around the village houses, dubbing it the Albanian Venice.

Have a coffee in the centre and take in the old houses, cobblestones and beautiful vibe. There is a 180 year old church you can also opt to take a look at.

ILLYRIAN ROYAL TOMBS

The Illyrian royal tombs are located in the village of Selcë e Poshtme. This is home to ancient royalty! From the 4th to the 1st centuries BC this was home to the best of the best, making it an important economic and political hub.

The tombs are UNESCO protected and built within the residing hill. These tombs are hardly visited by anyone which is a real shame.

There is no admission charge so take in the ancient history for free!

POGRADEC

WHERE TO EAT

If you're looking for a good restaurant to try within Pogradec then try The Change. This is a great contemporary fish restaurant that offers the fish 'Koran' which I talked about earlier.

WHERE TO STAY IN POGRADEC

There are many great affordable hotels to stay in in the city. The top three hotels are:

- Hotel Millennium
- Perla Hotel
- Hotel Enkelana

As Pogradec is a resort town, there are plentiful hotels here. If you're looking for a more Vila type accommodation rather than a large hotel, then try Vila Sigal.

KRUJA

HOW TO GET TO KRUJA

It only takes 45 minutes from the capital of Tirana. To get to Kruja by bus you need to go to the bus station called Stacioni Autobusave Zona e Veriut.

The bus costs around 100lek and departs at multiple times per day but, keep in mind this is Albania and bus times change regularly so it's best to ask a local when you are in Tirana.

If travelling by car you can park at the carpark just above the bazaar and walk. The old town is very small so it's easily walkable. There are barriers for cars in front of the road to the castle which open at 6 pm and closes again in the morning.

You could easily do Kruja as a day trip as there's not a whole lot to see and do but I recommend staying at least the night. Kruja is a beautiful place to relax in the mountains for some time away!

THINGS TO DO

Kruja also known as the city of Skanderbeg, a national hero for Albania, is a historic city and one that shouldn't be missed if you decided to travel to Albania.

Only 30km away from the bustling and busy capital of Tirana is a great spot for a getaway for some peace and quiet. I instantly fell in love with this place as it's located high in the mountains and gives you a chance to dive deep into Albanian history. Oh, and the antique shops and markets will pull you in if the history doesn't!

The city sits over 600meters above sea level and from the top, you gain the most picturesque panoramic views.

VISIT SKANDERBEG CASTLE AND MUSEUM

You simply must visit Skanderbeg castle. They also have a museum attached where you can learn more about Skanderbeg and the history of this castle and its surroundings. Entry is 200lek.

Skanderbeg was a national hero in Albania as he battled against the Ottomans and stopped them from taking over Albania.

From the castle, you get magnificent views of the city and mountains.

WANDER THE BAZAAR (PAZARI I KRUJËS)

Visit the bazaar located in the old part of town next to the castle.

This market dates back to the 14th century and has a wonderful selection of things to buy. Homemade rugs and carpets, traditional clothing, silver and copper objects, handmade wooden articles and an abundance of antique shops filled with interesting knickknacks.

You will want to buy nearly everything you see so make sure to take some cash with you!

WHERE TO EAT

There are many great places to sit down and have a great bite to eat. A restaurant meal in Kruja is extremely affordable.

My recommendation is Emiliano Restaurant. They do homemade food within castle walls. I talk more about Emiliano below!

Restaurant Bardhi is also a great choice and it is one of the oldest restaurants in the area as it opened in 1994!

Panorama Restaurant hosts an incredible view of the city as well as delicious traditional local food!

WHERE TO STAY IN KRUJA

The only place I recommend (because it's the best) is Emiliano Rooms.

Located within the castle grounds is a 400-year-old house which is also accommodation. At sunset, this is the best spot in my opinion! Grab a drink and take in the serenity and quietness of Kruja. They do fantastic food here too, I was blown away by the breakfast.

I have to say, the staff were a real highlight, they were incredibly friendly and helpful!

SHKODËR

THINGS TO DO

From Tirana, you can catch the bus or drive to the northern city of Shkoder. Shkoder is a charming city and a gateway into the Albanian Alps. You will love the north if you are more into the mountains than the beach.

There are a lot of things you can do in Shkoder including visiting Rozafa Castle. If you like museums then you can check out the Shkoder history museum, the site of witness and memory (which is set in a communist prison) or the Marubi Photography museum.

Shkoder is referred to as the cultural capital as the history is incredibly rich and you have the opportunity to learn a lot about the country with the various museums.

ROZAFA CASTLE

This 9th century BC castle was constructed by members of the Illyrian tribes and I have to say, this was one of the most magical castles I have visited. It overlooks the city of Shkoder as well as Lake Skadar. The Rozafa castle has an interesting legend that comes with it.

The legend goes something like this; 3 brothers were building the castle however, the castle kept falling. Suddenly a wise man appears and tells the brothers that the only way to keep the walls up was to put one of their wives into the walls. The brothers' wives would bring their husbands' lunch each day and they decided that the first wife to turn up with lunch the following day would be sacrificed and placed in the wall.

However, the 2 older brothers warned their wives about the plan when they got home. So the next day the wife of the younger brother turns up with lunch and she was the one to be sacrificed. But she did it on one condition. One of her eyes had to be exposed so she could watch over her newborn son, one breast had to be exposed so she could feed him and one hand had to be exposed so she could touch him. The castle was named Rozafa after her.

THINGS TO DO

WANDER THE OLD TOWN

Shkoder's old town is like no other in Albania. The architecture is extremely unique which is why I highly recommend that the best way to see and experience Shkoder is just by having a walk around and getting lost. There are plenty of great cafes you can stop by for a session of people watching and taking in beautiful views.

BIKE AROUND LAKE SKADAR

Upon arriving in Shkoder you will notice that nearly everyone in the city is biking! Shkoder has a huge biking culture so a fantastic activity during your stay is to hire a bike and travel to the nearby Lake Skadar to enjoy the surrounding nature.

GET A TATTOO IN A BUNKER

Want to get a tattoo to remember your time in Albania? How about getting a tattoo in an old bunker? It's no secret that Albania is full of Bunkers from the communist era, and some locals have decided to turn these concrete eye soars into something beautiful. The tattoo parlour is located in Bajze, a small town not far from the city.

SHKODER HISTORY MUSEUM

If you would like to learn more about the history of Shkodra, a trip to the Shkoder history museum can be a great idea. The building dates back to the early 1800s and became a museum in 1996. Here you can catch a glimpse of the culture.

DO A TRIP TO THETH OR VALBONA

Shkodra is known for being the start or finishing point for exploring the nearby Albanian Alps. If you have enough time on your trip I highly recommend visiting Valbona, Theth or both if you can, as they are both incredibly scenic parts of Albania that many dream to visit. If you would like to learn more about Theth Or Valbona, flick to their sections within this guide!

MESI BRIDGE

Mesi bridge is the largest bridge in Albania leftover from the Ottoman Empire. You can opt to do a bicycle tour from Shkodra as it's only a 15km ride to the bridge.

SHOKDER

WHERE TO EAT

There are so many great places to eat in Shkoder, especially if you wander around the old part of the city.

For Albanian food make sure you visit Vila Bekteshi, Fisi Restaurant or Tradita Geg & Tosk. For Italian food like pizza and pasta try out Fontana.

WHERE TO STAY IN SHOKDER

One of the most recommended places to stay in Shkoder is Hotel Tradita. This hotel is decorated like a traditional Shkoder home so you feel like you're stepping back in time!

If you're looking for a great hostel to stay in, I highly recommend Wanderers hostel. It's a fun place to stay centred in the old part of the city so it's in an incredible location.

THETH

THINGS TO DO

Theth is not to be missed on any trip to the Albanian Alps. You may have seen photos of this small village with the stone church and the alps in the background. It's undoubtedly one of the most beautiful places to visit in Albania, and in the Balkans.

I highly recommend staying at least 2 nights to get the most out of the area. There's a lot of beautiful things to do in Theth.

VISIT THE CHURCH

The famous church of Theth is a must-visit and inevitability you will see it as Theth is very small! Theth church has possibly the most beautiful backdrop a church has ever had.

The church was built in 1892. In 1917 the church was used as a school for the children in Theth to learn reading and writing.

BUY A LOCAL SOUVENIR

Upon my exploration of Theth, we came upon a woman shepherd who was multitasking and not only looking after her heard but also knitting pupa, which is a sort of sock but is thicker, more like a fabric slipper. It was the perfect souvenir to take home from Theth, and, I was highly underprepared and didn't bring anything warm. We visited in October!

VISIT THE BLOOD FEUD TOWER (LOCK-IN)

If you haven't heard about the infamous Albanian blood feuds, then you're missing out on a key part of northern Albania's history.

Blood feuds started as far back as the 15th century when the law of kanun came into play for the tribes in northern Albania and some other countries within the Balkans. The kanun states that when blood is taken the only way to solve is to take that of who stole the blood. Meaning if you murdered someone, the family of who has been murdered has the right to kill you and any of your (male) family members. It's basically a revenge law.

This tower is where men would hide, it was a sort of safe house where you couldn't be touched. Believe it or not, although this law is old, over 300 families in Albania still live in fear to this day and don't leave their homes because of blood feuds and the fear of being killed.

NEARBY HIKES

BLUE EYE HIKE

Distance: 12 miles (19.3km)
Hours: 6- 7 hours
Difficulty level: Medium

One of the best things to do in Theth is to visit the blue eye (Syri i Kalter). Don't get it mixed up with the one in the south of Albania, they are different!

Visiting the Blue Eye is a great thing to do for the day. The hike takes around 3 hours and is medium difficulty.

The hardest bit is the last hour, other than that the path is flat most of the way. There is an option to get a ride for most of the way and then you will need to walk for around 45 minutes to 1 hour. I walked there and got a ride back with some friends which I am so happy I did because after 3 hours (and preparing for the big hike the next day) it was a great option for an amateur like me!

There is a couple of restaurants/cafes at the start of the entrance of the blue eye (around the 2-hour walking mark). Don't be fooled like I was and think that you are nearly there when you still have another 1 hour to go with nearly all of it uphill.

NEARBY HIKES

THETH WATERFALL

Hours: 45 minutes from Theth church
Difficulty level: Easy/Medium

This is a great thing to do for a couple of hours. The Theth waterfall is not too far from the centre of Theth and it's a beautiful walk. The uphill stage of the walk only lasts around 15 minutes so it's not too bad and totally worth it when you reach the bottom of the waterfall.

NEARBY HIKES

THETH TO VALBONA HIKE

Distance: about 10.5 miles or 17 km
Hours: 6- 8 hours
Difficulty level: Medium

The most popular hike within Albania and often referred to as 'the hike' by other backpackers, the Theth to Valbona hike (or Valbone to Theth, whichever way you want to do it), is not to be missed and truly is one of the best things to do in Albania. I am not a hiker at all, but I do enjoy walking and I found this hike to be medium-difficult.

The last hour was the hardest (coming from Theth) as it's all uphill and it can be steep in some places with it feeling like it may never end. Or this could simply be me complaining a little too much.

The distance may vary a lot depending on where you stay. You could easily add another hour onto the walking time depending on where your hotel is, which is why you will hear about this hike so many different times.

We stayed near the church of Theth and left our hotel at around 8.20, and arrived at our Valbona hotel at 4.45 pm so it took us just over 8 hours to complete. We stayed at one of the first hotels in Valbona which I am thankful for too. Depending on where you stay, it may also add another hour walk on the road to your guest house!

There are a few cafes along the walk where you can buy drinks and fill up your water bottle. Make sure you bring some food with you. Often the guesthouses will offer to pack you a lunch for the hike so ask your guesthouse about this!

WHERE TO EAT

One of the best places we ate at was Guesthouse Sphella. It's great food, very affordable, and is run by a super friendly family. We got a big grill platter each which was only €7. The soup is only €2! After a trip to the blue eye or the waterfall make sure you stop here to fill up on yummy food.

WHERE TO STAY IN THETH

BUJTINA POLIA

This is where we stayed for 2 nights and I highly recommend it. We had a little cabin which was nice and cozy. It's located right next to the Theth church and about a 20-minute walk to the centre of Theth (where the mini market is). The family were friendly, and the food was good. Breakfast was a buffet and was filled with all the right things to prepare for a day of hiking.

We also had lunch there (*500lek pp*) which was a range of dishes like meat, cheese, salad, soup, bread, and water.

They have family-style dinners which were €10 per person. There was a lot of food and a typical Albanian style of lots of different dishes, so you get a bit of everything.

VALBONA

THINGS TO DO

Valbona is a small village nestled at the bottom of the Albanian Alps. It's a hot spot for tourists looking for a break in nature and to explore one of the most beautiful parts of the country. In the winter, the village is blanketed in snow, and in the summer international and local tourists flock here to do the famous hike which I talked about in the Theth section.

Valbona is much easier to access than Theth, making it more popular and more accessible for many. The history in this part of Albania is rich so if you can strike up a conversation with an English speaking local, you will hear many trials and tribulations of the region.

How to get to Valbona: Unlike Theth, Valbona is very accessible as there is a tar sealed road all the way to the village. Valbona sits right on the border of Montenegro and nearby Kosovo so if you can, make a plan to visit the countries nearby too, you won't be disappointed!

LAKE KOMAN FERRY

The most beautiful boat ride I have ever done was this one, and that's coming from someone who lives on the Albanian Riviera so that's saying something.

All of the bookings can be done on their website. The company will pick you up from your hotel in Shkoder and drive you to the ferry port of Koman which takes around 1 hour and 30 minutes. Then you will catch the ferry which takes 3 hours. Once you have arrived at the ferry port of Fierze you will then catch the last shuttle to Valbona which takes around 1 hour. If you are in Valbona and want to get back to Skhoder it's the same trip but in reverse.

This whole journey costs 20 euro or 2800 lek and takes around 6 hours (by the time you wait for the shuttles etc). All of this can be booked online or by giving them a call. You must make an advanced booking; it cannot be made on the day. You can choose to pay online (note that you will only pay for the ferry online, you will pay for the shuttles in cash), or it can all be paid in cash.

I highly recommend doing this trip, it was incredible to cruise over the artificial lake of Koman with the mountains on either side!

THINGS TO DO

VISIT THE OLD MILL OF VALBONA

One of the most popular things to do in Valbona is to walk to the west of the village where the old corn mill of Valbona is situated.

This mill is over 300 years old and is a great visit to gain an inside perspective on local life here in Valbona.

HIKE TO XHEMES' LAKE

You simply cannot visit this region unless you do a hike and the Xhemes lake hike is a beautiful beginner walk!

The trail starts near the old mill. You will walk roughly 220 meters through the forest until you get to the lake.

Make sure you are always following the red and white markings on the rocks which indicate the route.

HIKE TO THETH

This is usually the number one reason for tourists to visit Valbona. The hike to Theth is absolutely stunning. If you would like to find out more about it, flip to the Theth section of this guide where I go into depth about the hike.

This hike can get busy in the summer since it's one of the best things to do in Albania. I was surprised when I did it (beginning of October) that around 40 people were doing the hike also. I can imagine in the summer that this trail would get busy as it is the most popular hike in Albania after all and on so many people's bucket lists!

WHERE TO EAT

There is plenty of guest houses where you can eat within Valbona. I really enjoyed the restaurant at Hotel Margjeka, where we also stayed. The meals that we had there were incredible, affordable and hearty for the colder weather.

It's rated one of the top restaurants within Valbona too!

WHERE TO STAY IN VALBONA

I would highly recommend staying at **Hotel Margjeka** because it's one of the closest hotels to the start of the trail in Valbona. They also have a delicious breakfast which is included and it's one of the best restaurants in Valbona.

The room has a beautiful view and they had superb heating which was essential for October. The staff were super helpful and friendly too!

LEZHE

THINGS TO DO

Lezhe is not an obvious choice for tourists but it should be because it's slowly becoming a tourist destination and is one of the best cities in Albania. The city is famous because the national hero, Skanderberg was buried here.

Within the city, you can go visit the tomb of Skanderbeg along with his helmet and sword. If you want to relax in the sun then take a look at Shengjin Beach, a sandy beach only 8km from the centre. Nearby there are also sand dunes if you're feeling like a bit of adventure.

LEZHE CASTLE

The Lezhe castle which was built in Llyrian times is perched on the hilltops overlooking the city. The castle is a melting pot of architecture due to its many rises and falls. You can see Illyrian, Roman, Byzinate and Ottoman styles throughout.

If history and castles are really not your things, you should at least make the trip up there because the views from the castle are just incredible.

MRIZI I ZANAVE AGROTURIZËM

If you love food then you should learn more about Albania's slow food movement. Albanian food is becoming increasingly popular because the ingredients are usually grown organically and the flavours and fresh, simple but delicious. Mrizi i Zanave Agroturizëm is a must-see place.

It is notably one of the best restaurants in the country and has been featured on many TV programs, one featuring the famous British chef Rick Stein.

THINGS TO DO

TOMB OF SKANDERBURG

The tomb of the Albanian National hero Skanderberg, or formally known as Gjergj Kastrioti, was laid to rest within the 14th century St. Nicholas Cathedral. Although here is the tomb of Skanderbeg, his bones are not located here. 10 years after Skanderbeg died, a group of Ottoman soldiers came and took his bones, made them into small pieces while covering them with gold or silver, and used them for Talismans because they believed that if they had a piece of Skanderbeg they would be strong just like him.

RANA E HEDHUN

Did you know that Albania has dunes? Located only 3-4 kilometres from Shengjin, Rana e Hedhun is a beach that not many know about to this day.

The sand from the beach has escaped up the mountain making it a perfect location for sliding down the slope.

Bring a piece of cardboard so you can slide down the dunes with ease.

Shengjin Beach

Shengjin beach is a popular destination for Albanian tourists and some international travellers too. It's both a beach and a port!

The beach itself is unique to Albania as it's surrounded by pine forests and a mountain backdrop. Plus the beach is actually sand, which is hard to come by in

Albania as most beaches are usually pebbles.

FIER

THINGS TO DO

Although Fier is not exactly a tourist destination I would necessarily recommend, Fier does have one of the most important archaeological sites in all of Albania.

The city itself is nothing special and I wouldn't recommend staying the night in Fier, but it's a great day trip as Apollonia, one of Albania's largest archaeological sites, is only 20 kilometres from the city.

APOLLONIA

Apollonia was an ancient Greek city and is located right on the Vjosa banks. The city was built by Greek colonizers on the lands of the Taulantii Illyrian tribe. This archaeological park has been preserved well, however, only 5% of it has actually been excavated.

When you visit you will see how shocking that is because there is so much to see and the thought that only a small fraction has actually been dug is mind-blowing. During the 4th century AD, Apollonia was an important economic and trade centre.

How to get to Apollonia: There is a road leading all the way up to Apollonia so you can take your car. There's ample parking also.

If you want to take public transport you can take the Fier-Pojan Bus line, but keep in mind that the last trip is at 2:30 PM.

I would recommend during the summer getting here early as it can be very hot and also this is a popular destination for big tourist buses.

LIBOHOVË

THINGS TO DO

You won't see much about Libohove in guide books because many don't know this place exists which is such a shame because it's one the most beautiful places.

Despite it being a small place, it has a rich history and a stunning fortress! Libohove makes a great trip if you have a car and are travelling from Saranda to Gjirokastra or vice versa as the turn off it just before you hit the UNESCO city of Gjirokastra.

VISIT THE CASTLE

Ali Pasha is a name you will hear again and again and that's because he ruled Albania but was later killed by the Ottoman Empire.

Ali Pasha's sister married one of the most important families in Libohove and the castle was the dowry that she was given when she got married.

You can also visit the grave of Ali Pasha's sister as she was buried in Libohove

VISIT THE 4TH CENTURY TREE

This tree is one of the highlights of this small place as it dates back to the 4th century, which means it may be one of the oldest trees in the entire country.

WHERE TO EAT

There are a few cafes in the area and one restaurant which is located at the base of the tree. However, this is not always open so keep that in mind!

WHERE TO STAY IN LIBOHOVË

There is only one guest house and one hotel in the town of Libohovë. In my opinion, you are much better to stay in nearby Gjirokastra and make Libohovë a day trip instead of staying there as there are much more options for food and activities there.

CAPE OF RODON

CAPE OF RODON

If you're visiting the city of Tirana, a day trip must be made to the unique Cape of Rodon. Only a 1-and-a-half-hour drive from the bustling capital of Albania you can visit the serenity that is the largest cape in Albania.

Not only is the views stunning but you will be delighted by the 14th-century Rodoni Castle and the idyllic St. Anthony Church.

HOW TO GET TO THE CAPE OF RODON

The Cape of Rodon is only a 1 and a half-hour drive from Tirana or just over 1 hour from Durres. The road is in pretty good condition, with a few potholes here and there but that's Albanian roads for you. You will go through some beautiful villages and be blessed with some lovely views along the way.

In addition to driving, you can also easily hitchhike or join a tour group headed to the Cape of Rodon. If you drive there is plenty of space for parking. It's safe to leave your car there and walk to the cape from there.

You can't drive right up to the cape. You have to walk for around 500 meters to reach Rodoni Castle and the cape. The walk is easy enough. Along the way, you will also see bunkers built into the hill from the time of communism. They are slowly being taken over by nature and you might not even notice them!

THINGS TO DO

RODONI CASTLE

Rodoni Castle (also called Skanderbeg Castle) used to be surrounded by 4 defence towers and it has been noted in history that this castle was used as a piracy port or a transportation place for grain to nearby Ishmi.

These days Rodoni Castle is in ruins, but you can still see the arches and walls which remain and are preserved. It has been proved that there once was an ancient Illyrian settlement here too.

If you have time, take a walk along the Cape of Rodon at sunset for phenomenal views of Rodoni Castle and the rest of the coast.

THE CHURCH OF ST ANTHONY

Another main attraction in the Cape of Rodon is the St Anthony Church. This church was built in the same period as Rodoni castle and is very well preserved.

In fact, inside the church, you can still see a painting of a two-pronged eagle and a man on a horse. Because of that, this is one of the most popular churches to visit in Albania, not only for history but because of where it's placed as it has a magnificent view!

Today St Anthony's Church and the surrounding area are still considered sacred and every year locals and tourists join for festivities and pilgrimage. This is done on the 13th of June every year.

SOAK UP THE NATURE ON THE CAPE

Not only are you surrounded by incredible history but the nature along the Cape of Rodon is something else. White sand beaches all along the Durres coast, pristine water and a place to camp if you do want to stay in this beautiful part of Albania to soak it up, I know I would!

It's a unique part of the country as many beaches in Albania are stone, so having a sandy beach is a luxury in my eyes! If you want a more typical Albanian beach experience, Durres beach is nearby.

WHERE TO STAY IN CAPE OF RODON

As I said previously, you are welcome to freedom camp here. There are a few villas for rent on the Cape of Rodon, but no hotels. If freedom camping isn't your thing, you can stay further along the coast at one of the hotels in Durres.

If you do freedom camp on the cape, or just have a nice fire on the beach you MUST take all your rubbish with you. Dumping your rubbish is unacceptable and disrespectful to the land. Cape of Rodon has ongoing issues with people dumping their plastic etc on the cape. So, if you see anyone do this, I would recommend educating them about why they shouldn't do so.

LLOGARA NATIONAL PARK

THINGS TO DO

Within the Ceraunian Mountains lies one of the most beautiful parks and viewpoints of the country, Llogara National Park. The park was established in 1966 to protect the important ecosystems and biodiversity that it holds. In the summer, the park is cool making it a nice refreshing getaway. In the winter, the park is covered with snow while it looks over the Albanian Riviera.

NATIONAL PARK

One of the best things to do is to explore the park itself.

There are several walking trails that you can opt to do. Along the main road are restaurants, cabins and hotels.

The national park has the most incredible view if you are coming from Dhermi and heading into the park.

Just before you drive into the dense forest, be sure to stop over and take a minute for the view.

GRAMA BAY

Grama Bay is one of the most incredible looking beaches in Albania, there's just one catch. This beach can only be accessed by a long walk (over 8 hours) or by boat.

Located in Karaburun National Park, this is a newly discovered Albanian beach and because it's so secluded it's a great option and a must-visit. However, this won't last for long as many boats and tours are already starting to get a taste of Grama Bay. There are also some other incredible Albania beaches in Karaburun National Park but to access them you will need a boat or a good pair of hiking shoes and camping equipment.

PALASE BEACH

Palase beach is definitely in the top 3 most beautiful Albania beaches.

Right before you go on the Llogara pass through the national park is Palase beach, one of the most secluded beaches.

WHERE TO EAT

There are a few different restaurants you can check out if you do stay within the national park. My recommendation is Andoni Hotel Restaurant.

They do good food at reasonable prices. As it can sometimes be a bit cooler in the park, take the opportunity to try out some of the heartier dishes like meat with rice and the various stews.

WHERE TO STAY IN LLOGARA

There are not too many options when it comes to accommodation in Llogara National Park. The top 3 hotels in the park are Llogara Tourist Village, Hotel Alpin and Hotel Restaurant Alberti.

DHERMI

THINGS TO DO

The beach paradise of Dhermi is perfect for a holiday in the sun. Dhermi has become increasingly popular as the beaches here and nearby are beautiful. The village of Dhermi itself is charming, you could easily spend a few days soaking up the sun and partaking in some adventure activities.

DRYMADES BUNGALOW

If you're in Dhermi be sure to check out Drymades beach and have a drink at Drymades Bungalow. They have a super cool bar with bean bags and fairy lights right on the beach. It's one of the best hangout spots in the area and one of the best places to visit in Albania.

PIRATES CAVE

If you go to Dhermi, you simply cannot visit and not go to take a look at Pirates Cave. A famous Albanian writer Petro Marko wrote a beautiful book about Pirate's cave because it was so beautiful. If you visit the cave, you will also notice the pink cliffs which are incredibly unique.

The location is a natural wonder. The caves are located below the Monastery of St. Todhri. If you are a professional rock climber you can access it from above otherwise you can take a boat from Dhermi or Jale.

VISIT GJIPE

Whilst in Dhermi make sure to check out the beautiful beach of Gjipe. It's one of the best in Albania!

You can reach Gjipe by car to the nearest car park and then a 40-minute walk down to the beach.

Otherwise, rent a kayak or take a boat tour to explore it. As it's not accessible by normal car it means it's not visited by the masses so even in the height of summer you can chill down there and easily find a sunbed.

I talk more about Gjipe further in this guide!

WHERE TO EAT

There are some incredible restaurants and beach bars to check during your time in Dhermi. Here are some of the best recommendations:

- Alevra (Fantastic seafood and has a beach bar too)
- The Yacht Club
- Aloni Restaurant
- Luciano (one of the most popular places to eat in the area and very worth it!)
- Bia Bungalows (Amazing seafood & affordable)
- Piratet 1 (Great pizza at an affordable price)

WHERE TO STAY IN DHERMI

Luxury Accommodation

Elysium Hotel: This hotel is a luxury accommodation option that has a swimming pool, shuttle service right down to the beach and friendly staff. It's located just above Dhermi Beach, so you get the view of the beach as well as the mountains above.

Mid-cost

Drymades bungalow: This is the place to be during the summer. With fantastic accommodation options including bungalows, wooden rooms and stone rooms, friendly staff and a fun vibe throughout. Highly recommended!

Budget

Nino's Guesthouse: This place has a great view and only a 3-minute walk to the beach. It's affordable and the staff are incredibly friendly.

VUNO

THINGS TO DO

The village of Vuno has got to be one of the most picturesque villages on the whole Albanian Riviera. There are 200 homes within Vuno, and you will notice that they mostly all have orange roofs and orange windows!

Recently Vuno was made over as part of the 100 villages project. The project is aimed to help 100 villages within Albania improve infrastructure and develop tourism in these areas.

ST. SPIRIDON MONASTERY

This monastery sits in the centre of the village and was built in 1777.

It's a cultural monument within the village and is currently undergoing some restoration.

CHURCH OF ST. MARY OF MESODHIA

A few metres above the main road that winds through Vuno, is the church of St. Mary of Mesodhia.

When you enter you will notice the wall paintings, which were done in 1783. The church is in great condition as it's been preserved over the years.

VISIT THE NEARBY BEACHES

You simply cannot stay in Vuno and NOT explore the nearby beaches; it really would be a crime. There are plenty of beaches to visit, one including Gjipe. I highly recommend visiting this beach paradise. You can opt to hike to Gjipe which is a total of 5km. Bear in mind that the trail is sometimes hard to see so in parts you might be winging it, but it will be worth it once you get there!

Jale is another beautiful beach located not far from Vuno. This is yet another beach paradise located within the Albanian Riviera.

VUNO

WHERE TO EAT

There is only a couple of official places to eat in Vuno, remember that this village is tiny! So, if you stay here, you may be eating at the same place again and again. The best restaurant to eat at is Villa Filip Restaurant.

WHERE TO STAY IN VUNO

Vuno Hostel: If you're a backpacker you'll be pleased to know that there is a hostel in Vuno called Vuno Hostel. Prices start at 1200lek per night, per person!

Villa Filip: This Villa has beautiful views of the Riviera below. The staff are friendly and it's a great peaceful place to stay in the village of Vuno.

JALE

THINGS TO DO

Jale is a small hidden gem within the Albanian Riviera known for its crystal-clear waters. You can reach Jale by driving along the coastal road, as it's nestled between Himare and Gjipe.

Jale is the perfect location for a beach getaway because there's an array of activities to do here and nearby too. It makes the perfect base for exploring some of the best spots within the Albanian Riviera.

How to get to Jale

There's no public transportation to the beach, unfortunately, however, you can take the bus from Vlore to Himare and be asked to be dropped off at the entrance of the road leading to Jale. To walk down to the beach is around 5km so that will take you an hour. Hitchhiking is extremely popular in Albania so you could try asking one of the cars heading towards the beach to give you a ride.

The road to Jale is tar sealed so if you do have a car, you will have no problem driving right down to the beach.

Alternatively, you could catch a taxi from Vuno, which is the nearest village or from Himara. The drive from Himara takes around 20 minutes.

WALK TO AKUARIUM BEACH

The hidden beach of Akuarium can be reached by walking around 20minutes. You will need to walk past hotel Nuanti north to reach the secret beach.

Make sure you bring water and snacks as this is a virgin beach with no facilities.

RENT A KAYAK AND EXPLORE THE HIDDEN LOCATIONS

If you love an adventure and you want to explore the hidden parts of Jale and the soundings, then opting to hire a kayak is a fantastic idea. You can rent them on Jale beach for around 400lek per hour.

If you kayak north, towards Gjipe you will come across many hidden beaches, one being Plazhi Me Shpella. Be on the lookout for caves too, there's Mermaids Cave, Pirates Cave and Figs Cave.

You can easily kayak to Gjipe too which is one of the most beautiful beaches in the Albanian Riviera and a favourite for the locals. The distance is around 4 kilometres which should take you around 45minutes to reach, depending on how many times you stop to take a picture of the beautiful sites!

JALE

WHERE TO EAT

As Jale is a small place, there are not a whole lot of options for restaurants. Here are 3 that are recommended:

Restaurant Kapiteni: Fresh seafood and right on the beach!
Hotel Nuanti: This is a hotel, but they also offer a menu out on their patio.
Folie Marine Restaurant: This is a luxury hotel restaurant so you can expect to pay a little more, however, the food is great.

WHERE TO STAY IN JALE

There are not too many accommodation options in Jale as it is pretty small however here are the top ones you can check out.

Luxury accommodation**: Folie Marine Beach Hotel & club**

If you're looking for luxury, then this is it! This is one of the most beautiful locations for a hotel and the Folie Marine Beach hotel also offers 3 restaurants and swimming pool and everything you would need for a real beach getaway.

Mid-range: **Hotel Nuanti**

This hotel is closest to that secret beach I talked about on the last page. This accommodation is basic but meets all the needs of a summer getaway. The staff are incredibly friendly, and they serve delicious fresh seafood too!

Budget: **Social camping**

If you're on a budget and want an adventure, why not camp?! Social Camping Jal offers tents and also a bungalow if you fancy something a wee bit more luxurious. They do an incredible free breakfast here and the staff are friendly and always willing to help.

GJIPE

GJIPE BEACH

Gjipe beach is one of the most magnificent places to visit in Southern Albania. It's famous for its beautiful beach which can be accessed by a 40-minute walk, boat, or a 4×4. Let's get into how you can get to this beautiful paradise within the Albanian riviera!

HOW TO GET TO GJIPE BEACH

Depending on how you will reach Gjipe beach will depend if you will do it as a day trip or not. If you are doing the car/hike option, this can easily be a great stopover for the morning, afternoon or all day. Just make sure you leave before sunset as the road can get very dark!

BY BUS

You can easily reach the beach by car, bus, walking, boat and 4×4. If you want to reach Gjipe via bus you will have to ask the driver to drop you off at the entrance to Gjipe Beach. From there you will have to walk 2km to get to the carpark and from there you can descend to the beach (45min).

BY CAR

If you are travelling to Gjipe beach by car you can drive to the furthest point on the road to Gjipe where there is a small car park. From there you walk the trail which leads down to the canyon and eventually to Gjipe beach.

The walk takes approximately 45 minutes and goes past several bunkers and gives you plenty of beautiful views. The hike is relatively easy, but it is recommended that you wear sneakers to be safe as there can be some loose rocks as well as being a little slippery.

GJIPE BEACH

WALKING

If you are looking for a more active route to take then you can reach Gjipe beach by walking from Jale, Himara and Dhermi. Here's how:

Dhermi: The route is around 4km. There's a small trail that starts a little way out of the town from the main road.

Vuno: It is possible to walk to Gjipe beach from the small village of Vuno. The walk is 5km and you will have to do some wild hiking as the trail is not an obvious one and you may find yourself sort of winging it.

Jale: another way is to hike from Jal. Just ask one of the locals where the trail begins!
Use Maps.me for the best navigation via your phone.

BY BOAT/KAYAKING

Gjipe beach is a popular spot that is often reached by hiring a boat or kayak from a nearby location. You can easily kayak from Himara, Dhermi or Jale and spend a few hours soaking up the sun on Gjipe beach as well as exploring the canyon.

4×4

Another way you can reach the beach is by a 4×4. The road is very narrow in some parts and if there is another vehicle coming you are screwed.

TOP TIPS

BRING SUNSCREEN

Although these days Gjipe beach is visited by many, you won't find mass sun-beds taking up the entirety of the beach. Make sure you're always sun protected. If you do want a sun-bed there is usually a few people renting them for around 500lek.

SWIM TO THE CAVES

Along the coast from Gjipe is numerous caves that you can swim to. Make sure you visit them in low tide and always keep an eye on when the tides come in otherwise you can get trapped.

BRING LOTS OF WATER

Make sure you bring your own water to stay hydrated, particularly if you have hiked all the way there in summer!

BRING CASH

In the summer there is usually one or two people setting up mini restaurants and selling drinks etc. So always bring some cash with you just in case you get peckish. If you're visiting out of season take some snacks with you!

CHECK OUT THE CANYON

Gjipe is famous because it's so unique and unlike any other beach in Albania. There is a Gjipe canyon walk which you can do but I do warn that you should have the ideal equipment for rock climbing and be confident with that sort of terrain.

VISIT A MONASTERY/ FORMER COMMUNIST PRISON WARD

From the beach, you can walk along the coast on a road which was an ex-military road to the monastery of Saint Theodore. The hike takes approximately 45 minutes. This monastery was used as a prison ward during communism but nowadays has been reconstructed.

WHEN TO VISIT

The most popular time to visit is summer as this is when most people visit the country but don't be afraid to visit out of season. I would advise you not to visit in winter because there may be flash flooding.

If you visit in May/June or Sept/Oct, you should be fine. Just keep an eye out for the weather.

Also, take note that the businesses who normally operate down there (restaurant/camping) probably won't be there out of season so be prepared to take everything yourself.

Another quick note is to always take care when exploring thick forests like in the canyon. Albania does have snakes so always be aware of where you are going and what your environment is like.

This also goes with visiting the caves and even hiking down to the beach. Always take care.

If you are going into the canyon, be aware of falling rocks. When I was there last, a boulder at the top of the canyon broke and fell to the ground which would have instantly killed anyone below.

WHERE TO STAY IN GJIPE

In the summer you can opt to camp at Gjipe beach if you're not planning on doing the hike back up to the car park. There is one place called Gjipe Eco Camping.

They provide you with a tent etc so you can stay down at Gjipe beach for the night and enjoy some star gazing!

You are also welcome to freedom camp there if you have all the gear yourself. There's plenty of room.

Just make sure you have all the essential equipment to set yourself up.

VLORA

THINGS TO DO

Vlora is one of the most important cities in Albanian history as this is where Albania claimed its independence from the Ottoman Empire at the start of the 20th century.

Vlora also makes a great city to stay in and it's a gateway to see many beautiful destinations nearby. The city is the northernmost point of the Albanian Riviera, with Saranda being the southern tip.

Vlora has some fantastic beaches nearby too. There is the main beach, although I wouldn't recommend swimming there because the water is kind of murky as there is a port. I highly recommend going south of the city, past the tunnel and here you can find some incredible beaches along the coastline.

KANINE CASTLE

Perched high on the hilltop above Vlora is Vlora castle which was constructed in the 4th century BC.

It sits 380 metres above sea level and has the most incredible view of the city below. Even if you're not into castles and history, at least come here for the stunning view!

INDEPENDENCE MONUMENT

Albania declared its independence from the Ottoman Empire in 1912 and you can visit the centrepiece that celebrates that!

The monument was constructed in 1972 and is located in Vlore's square. This is also a great location to grab a seat and people watch!

THINGS TO DO

MURADIE MOSQUE

This stunning Ottoman mosque survived the communist regime and is one of the religious buildings that stands today. The mosque was built by Mimar Sinan in 1537! Mimar was the Ottomans' leading architects and apparently, he even helped with the design of the Taj Mahal in India.

VISIT ORIKUM

Orikum is a small village located south of Vlora. There is an archaeological site here, however, you need special permission as it's located within a Navy Base. Orikum was the first place taken by Julius Caesar during his invasion of Epirus.

ZVERNEC MONASTERY

This is a must-see if you do visit Vlora as this place is like no other in Albania!

The island that this monastery sits on is located in the Narta Lagoon which is a protected site.

This is one of the most beautiful religious buildings in the south of Albania.

Not too many people know about this place still to this day!

VISIT SAZAN ISLAND

One of the best trips you can do is hop on a boat tour and visit Sazan island and Karaburun Peninsula. Sazan is a militarized island and during the cold war, it was home to chemical weapons and submarines. It is still used today but for a different reason, the fight against drug crime for the Albanians and Italians since it's so close to Italy. Up until 2017, Sazan Island was off-limits but today you are allowed to visit a small part of the island!

Before you visit you do have to register with the police in Vlora. The trip to Sazan costs 20 euro per person and go for around 6-8 hours depending on where you want to go. To organise go to the port of Vlora as there you can book your desired trip.

WHERE TO EAT

Piceri Restaurant Mustafa2: This restaurant is one of the best in Vlora and has delicious food with any dish you could ever ask for including seafood, pizza, pasta and more.

Tre Forchette Restaurant: This is one of the best restaurants in Vlora and one of the most highly recommended. The fresh seafood is delicious!

Restaurant Joni Vlore: If you're looking for a fine dining experience and some of the best seafood in the city this can be a great pick.

Summer depo: This is a great bar within Vlora with a nice vibe.

WHERE TO STAY IN VLORA

Regina Blu: This is one of the best luxury places to stay within Vlora. It has a beautiful view of the sea with an incredible pool and facilities.

Hotel Liro is also a popular option as it is located right within the cliff face with a private beach and friendly staff.

QEPARO

THINGS TO DO

The charming small village of Old Qeparo is one you will instantly fall in love with as I did. Along the Albanian Riviera, in between Borsh and Porto Palermo is one of the best places to see what a traditional village was like in Albania.

There are two parts to Qeparo, the lower and upper parts. The lower part of Qeparo has a beautiful beach and a few places to stay and relax if you want to be up and close to the sea.

The other part of Qeparo is the old upper village and is positioned on top of a mountain 300m above sea level.

UPPER QEPARO

Old Qeparo is incredibly fascinating to me as its half abandoned. It feels as if this village has been left behind yet the character that this place has is immense and there is huge potential for future tourism here. But it's one of those places you visit where you wish and hope that it stays exactly the same, so it doesn't lose any of its charm.

The village was pretty much abandoned in the 90's after the fall of communism in Albania. Many families moved to different locations and countries to survive. These days there are some people living there in the old original stone houses which have been preserved and re-done.

LOWER QEPARO

Lower Qeparo is a true summer destination. This small piece of paradise is home to a few hotels and restaurants, but the place is relatively small.

If you're looking for a quieter getaway along the Albanian Riviera, then this can be a great option!!

HOW TO GET THERE

The road to upper Qeparo can be taken by a turn off after/before the lower part of Qeparo. You drive for around 5-10 minutes up a windy road to reach the village.

Within the village itself, you cannot drive so you have to park your car near the centre and walk around.

WHERE TO STAY IN QEPARO

There are a few great places to stay within Upper Qeparo and new properties are being added every year as restorations continue.

You can stay at either Vila Leon, Les Villas de Qeparo or Villa Belvedere.

You can stay in the lower part of Qeparo as there are many beachfront properties. One of the best to stay in is **Hotel Riviera.**

PORTO PALERMO

THINGS TO DO

This picturesque bay is located just south of Himara and is a great stopover point. There's not a lot of activity here but there are a couple of great things to see before moving on. There is a sort of beach area where you can swim but it's not as big as many other beaches in Albania.

If you have a van, you could camp here. During the summer I have seen many people pulling up and making this location their home for the night as it's quiet and scenic.

CASTLE

The 19th-century castle that lies in the bay is also known as the castle of Ali Pasha. It's unique as the castle is a triangle shape that differs from every other castle in the country. I highly recommend coming here and exploring. Be prepared it's quite dark inside and kind of spooky but the top of the castle gives you a beautiful outlook to the Albanian Riviera.

If you look towards Himara you may see a concrete structure on the hillside. This is a submarine bunker from the communist era. You are not allowed to enter, however, if you had a kayak, you could see the entrance up close!

BEACHES NEAR THE CASTLE

There are some superb beaches and coves to swim nearby the castle. Highly recommend stopping here for an afternoon, or overnight if you have camping equipment.

LLIMANI BEACH

Just past the castle, about a 2minute drive and just before you get into Himara, is one of my favourite beaches along the riviera. It's called Llimani Beach.

There are a few beach bars here so you can enjoy the entire day swimming, eating and relaxing in the sun!

HIMARA

THINGS TO DO

Along the Albanian Riveria lies a small coastal town of Himara (Himare in Albanian). It's one of the must-see stops as it is more relaxed than the seaside city of Saranda and a perfect base to relax in without getting too bored.

There are plenty of things to do in Himare and lots of things to see nearby too. Still, Himara is one of my favourite go-to places and somewhere I always recommend tourists to stay for a night or three!

VISIT THE OLD CASTLE

Up in the hills, there is a beautiful village with a castle and a few accommodation options. The castle is worth a visit. You can catch a bus ride or walk.

The castle is ruined but it's still beautiful in my eyes. Within the castle walls are an old stone village and cobbled walkways. From the top, you gain stunning views over Himara.

The first time I visited Himara I stayed in this part and it was so peaceful!

ENJOY THE BEACHFRONT

Himara has a couple of great beaches - Livadi and Prinos. The city centre beach is nice, but I love the two other beaches in either city of the centre better.

EAT AT ENIGMA RESTAURANT

This is a great place to enjoy a bite to eat with a great view. This restaurant is located on the boulevard and does superb pizza! I can highly recommend the Italian here.

THINGS TO DO

ENJOY FRESH SEAFOOD

As you are in the Albanian Riviera you absolutely must try the seafood in Himare. Some good restaurants are Taverna Lefteri or Cibo Mare E Terra.

ENJOY A XHIRO ALONG THE BOULEVARD

A Xhiro means walk and this is something that you will notice all the locals do around sunset.

Not only in Himara but all over Albania the locals wake up from their afternoon naps and gather along the main boulevards around the country to catch up with friends and enjoy the beginning of the night.

HIRE A KAYAK AND GO TO THE SECRET BEACH 'GJIRI I FILIKURIT'

Just south of Himara centre is a beach known on google maps as Gjiri i Filikurit. It can be accessed by a dodgy walk and a bit of abseiling down a rope. Or you can catch a boat or a kayak!

DAY TRIPS FROM HIMARA

There are a lot of things to do near Himara too which is why many people make it a base to see nearby features.

1. Porto porlemo
2. Qeparo
3. Borsh
4. Jale
5. Gjipe Beach

WHEN TO VISIT

July and August are the busiest months in Albania. Slowly June and September are becoming busier too. If you come to Himara in the off-season, be aware that a lot of the restaurants and accommodation options are shut.

Along the boulevard, there are still restaurants open and it's definitely still possible to have a nice holiday. Just don't expect any wild parties and for the town to be buzzing. I prefer it in the off-season as it's incredibly peaceful!

WHERE TO STAY IN HIMARA

Backpackers: I recommend staying at Himara Downtown Hostel or Himara Hostel. Both are great options when visiting Himara.
If you are travelling with a friend/s it's sometimes even cheaper if you get a place to yourself using Booking.com.

When I came to Himara with 2 of my friends we rented a room for a total of €10 near the castle. It came with breakfast too, so it was cheaper for us than to stay in a hostel!

Mid-budget: There are lots of apartments and rooms to rent in Himara. I stayed just out of the centre called Villa Marine blue. My partner and I rented a room for 2000lek a night (in summer it's double). It was lovely, right on the beach and the owner is super lovely

Luxury Accommodation in Himara: There are a number of beautiful luxury accommodations in Himara including Scala Bungalows and Sea View Hotel.

FINIQ

FINIQ ARCHAEOLOGICAL SITE

This site is not usually recommended on usual lists because not a lot of tourists know about it! Finiq is an archaeological site that sits on the best vantage point overlooking the nearby region and the city of Sarande.

Finiq dates back to the 5th century BC.
You can see the remains of an ancient theatre, a small prostyles temple, Hellenistic houses, Byzantine church and other important relics and monuments.

Finiq is very unspoiled and amazingly they are still excavating it today and finding new information. I would highly recommend a trip from Saranda to Finiq.

Bring your lunch and spend a few hours walking around and taking in the history because it's truly amazing and very peaceful up there. Tickets cost 200 lek. You can get to Finiq by either driving, taking a taxi or hitchhiking.

PERMET

THINGS TO DO

Permet is still relatively an undiscovered gem but this location won't stay secret for long. Permet is home to some of the most beautiful natural scenes, interesting history and great food.

It's known as the city of roses as it is dubbed the cleanest and greenest city in Albania!

TASTE THE LOCAL FOOD

Permet is known for making great brandy, raki and fruit preserves which include one called gliko. Due to its positioning, the products from Permet are delicious. I highly recommend checking out one of the great restaurants here.

The first one I recommend is Familjari. We had an array of dishes like Fergese, grilled meat and more. The food was extremely good, all while being super affordable.

The next restaurant I recommend is Trifilia, where they again have great food at great prices. This is the most popular restaurant in the city, and it has a lovely balcony rooftop.

The staff are super friendly and helpful too!

BENJE HOT POOLS

This is one of the main reasons why people know Permet is because of these hot pools.

Now let me clarify, the pools are not hot, don't expect a steaming hot pool, they are definitely lukewarm but it's still worth it.

There is one big pool that has been artificially made and then they are several more, the further down the valley you walk.

Although the big one is the main attraction, I recommend checking out the smaller ones too!

LENGARICA CANYON

If you keep walking past the hot pools around 200 meters you will be in Lengarcia Canyon which is stunning. You can do a guided tour if you wish to go deep into the canyon.

THE BIG ROCK

Within the centre of the city, you will notice a giant rock which you can walk to the top of! I highly recommend doing this as you get a stunning view of the city and the Vjosa river. Even though you might be thinking it's just a rock, trust me the short walk up is worth it! At the top, there are also remains of some ruins that date back to the 4th century!

VISIT THE BROKEN BRIDGES

If you are going to and from Permet, look out for some interesting bridges along the way, we came across an array of broken, old bridges which made for fantastic photo opportunities. Be careful as many of them look like they are hanging on by a thread. But do be sure to look out for them during your travels!

KATIUT BRIDGE

This bridge was built by the Ottomans in the 19th century and is a real highlight when visiting the Benje hot pools. With many of the historic monuments, Ali pasha commissioned the Bridge, so it is also known as Ali Pasha Ottoman Bridge. Make sure you walk to the top, but I do have to warn you, be careful as the stones in the summer can be extremely slippery and you do not want to fall off.

BORSH

THINGS TO DO

The village of Borsh is a small village known for two things, its abundance of delicious olive oil and having the longest stretch of beach in Albania. This sleepy village deserves a stopover whether you're a history-lover or a beachgoer.

Borsh is only 32km from Saranda and the road on which the Albanian Riviera is situated is just stunning. Driving this road is one of the best things to do in Albania and is one of the most scenic drives in the world.

BORSH CASTLE

I highly recommend making a trip to Borsh castle which sits on the mountain overlooking the beach. The castle is in ruins, but it's often missed by tourists and is completely forgotten.

The views are stunning. There's also an old mosque on the castle walls. This was added by the Ottomans! It's not a working mosque as it's nearly completely ruined but it's beautiful inside and you can still see some of the paintings on the ceiling.

BORSH BEACH

One of the best places to go in Albania is Borsh.

Borsh is also very chilled and holds the longest stretch of beach in Albania, making it one of the best beaches in Albania!

It's situated in between olive groves and is a nice place to get away from the craziness of Saranda in the summer.

SARANDA

THINGS TO DO

Saranda is the most beautiful city to visit in Albania, no questions asked. There are many amazing things to do in Saranda (also called Sarande in Albania), such as lots of historical sites and eating all the delicious seafood dishes that you can find in Albania.

The Sarande beaches are also some of the most beautiful beaches of the Albania Riviera. In the summer months (July and August) the city is full, and the nightlife is the best in the country.

Spring and autumn are the best months to visit in my opinion as the city slows down and the prices lower because it's out of season.

RUINS IN SARANDE CENTER

Located in the centre of Saranda right next to the little park, are ancient ruins of a synagogue dating back to the 5th century. In the 6th century, these buildings were converted into a basilica but later were destroyed due to an earthquake.

Amazingly, these ruins were only discovered in 1984. You could visit these ruins within 15 minutes, there's nothing too exciting about the Sarande ruins unless you are really interested in ancient history but nevertheless they are still something you should look at while you're in the city.

You will also see other signs of ancient Saranda throughout the city. On the boulevard, you will discover a part of the ancient city walls.

LËKURËSI CASTLE

Overlooking the city of Saranda is Lëkurësi Castle. Unfortunately, Lëkurësi Castle has been turned into a restaurant these days but it's worth the trip because the view of Sarande's beaches is really amazing, especially at sunset.

Lëkurësi Castle itself was built in 1537.

You can easily walk from Saranda centre to Lëkurësi Castle if you're up for a bit of a hike, it takes around 45 minutes to reach the top of the castle.

THE MONASTERY OF THE 40 SAINTS

Many miss the opportunity to visit this historic site and a beautiful vantage point. This monastery is a special place, it was built between the 4-6th century and houses 40 rooms within. It was dedicated to the 40 Martyrs of Sebaste who refused to give up their Christian faith during the early stages of the Roman empire in Armenia, so they were locked in the building to die.

The monastery was in good condition up until 1944 when it was bombed by British soldiers who believed there was a German garrison hiding inside.

THINGS TO DO

KODRRA BEACHES

If you're looking for the best beaches in Saranda I recommend walking west of the city (past the ferry docks).

There two different Saranda beaches that I recommend, one is called Era beach and the other doesn't officially have a name but its where Cocktail Dreams (a beach bar) is situated.

I personally don't like the beaches in the centre as they can be a little dirty, but these Sarande beaches are nice and easy to get to, only max 20 minutes' walk from the centre!

MONASTERY OF SAINT GEORGE

Manastiri i Shën Gjergjit is another one of my favourite places not far from the city of Saranda, on the way to Ksamil. This 14th-century monastery sits on top of a hill and has a spectacular view. It's also in great condition and if you're lucky there will be a man there who can open the grounds for you so you can look inside.

The path to the Manastiri i Shën Gjergjit is not in great condition so beware if you are a little older because the surface isn't the best to walk on.

ST MARYS MONASTERY (KOSTAR)

If you have access to a car I highly recommend taking a trip to St Marys Monastery, located in a village called Kostar. The Monastery of St Mary is special because it is built within the cliff face! It's only around a 30-minute drive from Saranda to Kostar. The road is good enough to drive right to the top.

The view from Kostar is absolutely stunning as you can imagine and so is the building! You will not see Kostar recommended to tourists as most Sarande locals don't even know it exists.

THINGS TO DO

PLAZHI BARDENESH

Not far from Sarande's centre is a quiet little beach spot. Great for a sunset viewing or just to chill out. This Sarande beach is quite small but there are lots of places to swim not far from the beach too.

MONASTERY BEACH

After looking at St Georges Monastery (Manastiri i Shën Gjergjit) you should then take the road down to Monastery Beach. It's a small beach, but one of the best beaches in Sarande as it's really beautiful and quite enclosed. I think it's one of the most beautiful beaches in Saranda.

PULËBARDHA BEACH

Situated after Mirror Beach there is Pulëbardha which is a smaller yet just as beautiful Sarande beach. There's one restaurant here which serves great food.
There is a large rock on the beach considered its own attraction as there is a cave beneath it.

TAKE AN XHIRO AT SUNSET

Throughout the year the Sarande locals participate in an Xhiro. In Albania, a Xhiro is when the locals come out of their houses and walk, meet and socialise around sunset. During the summer months, Saranda's main boulevard is packed with people and it's a great way to get out and see the lively city!

MIRROR BEACH

After Monastery beach there is a beach call Mirror (or Plazhi i Pasqyrave in Albanian). This is another stunning Sarande beach and, in the afternoon, has some big waves which are always fun. Beware that the road for this beach is quite bad.

In the summer the beach is packed and the road to it is only really made for 1 car.

There are a lot of potholes so just be aware that you look at the road before making your way down, so you're not stuck halfway. The struggle of the road is worth it though because the colour of the water is crazy beautiful!

THINGS TO DO

BLUE EYE

Blue Eye is a natural phenomenon only 25 minutes from Saranda. Divers have tried to discover how deep the spring is but have only gone down 50 meters deep and to this day cannot find how far down the spring goes because the current is so strong! Usually, people spend an hour or two here. The water year-round is 10 degrees!

Visiting Blue Eye is one of my favourite things to do near Saranda because it is so pretty and unique.

WHERE TO EAT

Taverna Laberia: This little family-run restaurant, in my opinion, is one of the top places to eat in the city. It's located only a 15-minute walk from the centre. They do great souvlaki here as well as other grilled meat, salads and delicious tzatziki. I can recommend pork pancetta, greek salad, chicken on the spit, and open souvlaki.

Fishland: Just a 30-minute walk from the centre is the main fishing port for Saranda. This is where the fishing boats come in at sunset and bring in the fresh catch from the day. Near the port, there are a couple of fish restaurants, one being Fishland. It serves GREAT seafood at affordable prices.

Haxhi: Haxhi is one of the most popular places to eat for seafood lovers. They do good quality food at reasonable prices. Try the mussels there, they are some of the best in the city as well as the calamari and the spicey shrimps!

The Mussel House: The mussel house experience is a must if you're a seafood lover. You can not only eat fresh mussels at the restaurant but actually, take a boat tour to see the farms where they grow. Mussel house is between Saranda and Ksamil so you can either drive or take a taxi.

Wine Bar: This wine bar is a great spot for a glass of wine overlooking the city of Saranda. The location is stunning, right near the monastery of the 40 saints which is a personal favourite of mine. To get here you will most likely drive or catch a taxi. You can walk which I normally do when visiting the monastery but just keep in mind it's an uphill walk which will take you around 40-50 minutes!

Maria Magdalena: If you're a pizza lover like me then you will love Maria Magdalena. They do some of the best pizzas I have ever tasted. One of the reasons I love Albania is they have a big Italian influence which means they nail Italian food right on the head!

Old Story: Old Story is a restaurant with a Macedonian chef which means you can find a fusion between both cultures here. The food is absolutely delicious and so is the wine! If you're walking the boulevard, make a stop here for a bite to eat and you won't be disappointed.

Limani: This is by far one of the most popular places in Saranda and the biggest restaurant in the city. It's located right in the centre so it's easy to get to. They have a lot of different meals. From meat, pizza, pasta, salads, you name it they will probably have it. It's reasonably priced and right on the water so it's a nice setting too. If you want a 'commercial-style restaurant then visit Limani.

WHERE TO EAT

Manxurane: This is a french inspired restaurant that has some of the best contemporary food in the city. Here you can find items that you won't find on other menus in the city so if you are looking for a different food choice in Saranda, come visit this place!

Salad Farm: If you're vegan, vegetarian or you just love a salad and want to try something new, then try out Salad Farm. It's located near Santa Quaranta. They do a nice Chinese chicken salad, Falafel salad (my favourite) and Thai beef salad as well as smoothies!

Demi Lounge: Demi lounge has one of the largest menus in Saranda. I would highly recommend checking out this place at least once during your time in Saranda. It's also a great place to work from as they have power outlets outside and a beautiful view right on the water.

Paradise: This restaurant is located right at the end of the boulevard and sits right on the water. The dish I recommend trying here is the shrimp saganaki. It's the best I've tasted in Saranda!

Fish Filipi: If you're looking for local seafood at affordable prices then check out Fish Fillipi. This restaurant is super popular with the locals because of its delicious prices and good quality seafood.

Oxhaku: This is yet another great restaurant to try the local seafood at affordable prices. Oxhaku has a large seafood menu and something for everyone. Even if you're not into seafood they do have other options available like pork chops.

Taverna Kapiteni: Kapiteni is located next to the stadium of Saranda and has real local seafood. This is truly a local's restaurant with fresh seafood caught the day of. I highly recommend trying the calamari and risotto, it's some of the best!

Te Bequa: Te Bequa is a small restaurant that serves homemade Albanian food at local prices. This is not a tourist restaurant at all. If you want to try authentic food, come to this restaurant.

The Garden: This small restaurant sits right on the boulevard is also a great pick for authentic Albanian food at affordable prices. My top pick here is the fish soup!

NIGHTLIFE

Mango (Summer only): This is the most popular club located just out of the Saranda city centre. You will need to catch a taxi or hitchhike as it's quite a walk, especially if you're staying on the other side of the city. There is usually an entry fee (500 Lek). The whole city just about forms at mango on any given night during the summer. This is closed during the winter but usually opens back up on the 1st of May to celebrate the opening of the season.

Factory (Summer Only): This club is even further out of the city. It's essentially a huge warehouse with music.

Orange: This is located just a walk away from the boulevard. It's right on the beach, has good music and an easy option if you don't want to trek all the way to mango.

Jericho (Summer only): Right on the boulevard is Jericho which is famous for its cocktails. It serves a great view over the boulevard.

Rei Bar: This bar is nestled looking over the boulevard. There's a cool atmosphere, the drinks are good and it's a great place to come to chill out for a few drinks. There is a rooftop open in summer but in the winter you can have your coffee inside downstairs

21 Bar: This is a popular intimate hangout in the centre. Trendy bar with a cool ambience!

City lounge (summer only): This is another great bar which is a local favourite too. Right on the water and near Orange bar.

WHERE TO STAY IN SARANDA

Bougainville Bay: This hotel is the only hotel with a spa! Bougainville is a big resort located in the tourist section of Saranda. There are great beaches below and a great restaurant onsite as well as nearby.

Glow Boutique Hotel & Suites: This four-star boutique hotel is a perfect choice as it is kid-friendly. The rooms are affordable and each room has a flat-screen TV, desk, and a private bathroom.

Andon Lapa Suites: The services are high-end and cater to all the needs of the clients. The most common facilities in the hotel are free parking, a swimming pool, a beachfront location, an outdoor pool, free Wi-Fi, a bar, and family rooms.

BUTRINT

BUTRINT

Butrint is an ancient city that was inhabited since prehistoric times. This site was an important site with ancient artefacts found dating back to the iron and middle ages. You can see some artefacts in the museum which is located within the castle.

Within Butrint you will see very well-preserved ancient buildings such as a theatre which seats over 2500 people. It is still used from time to time for events.

There's also the Temple of Asclepius as well as an Acropolis, columns, a beautiful floor mosaic (includes medallions of 69 churches), a 6th-century basilica, Lions gate and a Castle with an incredible view of Lake Butrint and the surroundings.

You will see when wandering around Butrint that some of the buildings are still deep underground. There's still a lot to be discovered within the Butrint national park! Some locals believe that Butrint was actually the sunken city of Atlantis.

HOW TO GET THERE

By Car: Getting to Butrint is incredibly easy. If you have a car then you can drive here, there's a big parking lot next to Butrint. You just follow the road that goes from Saranda to Ksamil. When you will pass Ksamil and just keep driving until the road ends, that's Butrint! The ride takes about 20-30 minutes.

By bus: There's a bus which leaves every hour from Saranda (and goes through Ksamil too). The bus costs 150 lek from Saranda and will take you to the door of Butrint. From Saranda, the bus leaves from the small roundabout near the old fruit and vegetable market, or you can also catch it from the centre at the bus stop that's opposite the ruins and friendship park.

By taxi: There will be taxi drivers that can take you to Butrint easily for around 10 euros each way (about 1300 LEK).

COST OF BUTRINT

To get into Butrint you can buy tickets at the counter or online to save money. Check out their website for the updated prices.

OPENING HOURS OF BUTRINT

Butrint is open every day from 9am until dusk but the museum is open from 9am – 4pm.

TOP TIPS FOR VISITING BUTRINT

- **Go early!** In the summer temperatures can easily reach the late 30's/40 degrees Celsius. Even though Butrint is mostly covered in a dense forest it's still ideal to get in early to beat the crowds too. From April-September cruise ships dock in Saranda and the cruise ship passengers come here by busloads.

- **Wear comfortable shoes.** Butrint is a big park and most likely you will spend at least a couple of hours walking around.

- **Take water and snacks with you.** There's a restaurant at the top of the park but I always recommend taking something with you to keep you going, particularly water!

- **Go even further and take a picnic with you!** There are plenty of places to stop throughout the park to have a little picnic and enjoy the scenery.

- **Time your visit so you can see the mosaic of Butrint revealed!** Only a few days every year the mosaic which lies within Butrint is uncovered for the public to see. For the rest of the year, it is covered up with stones to preserve it. To see this incredible piece of history, make sure you check the Butrint site for details on when they will be uncovering it.

KSAMIL

THINGS TO DO

Ksamil is the most popular destination along the Albanian Riviera and for good reason – it's beautiful!

Sandy Ksamil beaches, clear water, fresh seafood and the perfect place to relax. There are so many wonderful things to do in Ksamil, Albania, you're sure to fall in love with this great city.

These days Ksamil has become increasingly popular with thousands of tourists flocking to this small paradise in the south of the country. I remember when I first arrived in Ksamil before moving to Saranda and I was in awe. I had no idea that Albania had a paradise this beautiful.

THE KSAMIL BEACHES

This is a given really. The beaches in Albania are some of the best in the world, and Ksamil beaches are the best of those. So not surprisingly a day at one of the beaches is one of the best things to do in Ksamil.

If you are staying in paradise you may as well enjoy it! Take a good book, rent out a sunbed and spend the day swimming, reading and enjoying the scenery. Sunbeds are rentable on most Ksamil beaches (approximately 1000lek).

If you don't like sunbeds, you should find yourself a nice, quiet spot on another nearby beach as the main beaches are usually full of beds. If you visit in the off-season you're going to be able to find a lovely spot on the main sandy beaches without having to pay for a sunbed.

THINGS TO DO

VISIT MONASTERY BEACH

This beach is in between Saranda and Ksamil but totally worth a visit. To get there, you can catch the bus that goes in between Ksamil and Saranda. The bus will let you out on the side of the road and from there you can walk up to the monastery or walk down to the beach.

I highly recommend looking at the monastery before the beach if you have time! It's really beautiful and the view from the top is incredible. Monastery beach is such a hidden gem.

MARVEL AT THE UNESCO SITE BUTRINT

Butrint is only a 10-minute drive from Ksamil, Albania and is a UNESCO World Heritage Site. It is one of the most unique Ksamil attractions! Butrint was an ancient city which first belonged to the Greeks, then the Romans and lastly bishopric in Epirus It will take 2 or 3 hours to explore and costs 1000 Lek entry.

You will want to visit in the morning or late afternoon as the sun can be overbearing in the summer, and you will appreciate it a lot more in the cooler weather. No matter when you visit, Butrint is one of the best things to do in Ksamil.

VISIT BLUE EYE (SYRI I KALTËR)

Located not too far from Ksamil lies a natural phenomenon. Some people think it's just another Ksamil beach, but Blue eye is a powerful spring that goes as deep as... well actually nobody knows because nobody has been able to dive that far down!

There's still no idea where this spring starts and the temperature stays at a cool 10 degrees (reminds me of New Zealand water!). This is one of the most popular Ksamil attractions, so in the summer this place does get busy!

WHERE TO EAT

Guvat – One of my favourite places to eat in Ksamil is Guvat. The seafood is delicious and it's a very romantic place to eat! It overlooks one of the main Ksamil beaches. It's a little expensive but the food is top quality.

Korali – Great seafood and always beautifully plated food! The staff are friendly and there's a great view of Ksamil, which is always a plus!

Brothers fish and meat tavern – Very affordable prices, quality food and all-around a solid place to eat in Ksamil, Albania. If you want value for money, then pick this restaurant.

WHERE TO STAY IN KSAMIL

Hotel Ardiani: This hotel is located right on the beachfront so if you want to sleep with the Ksamil beaches on your doorstep, then pick this hotel! There is a daily buffet breakfast, Free Wi-Fi, and an onsite restaurant too.

Abalone: One of my favourite Ksamil hotels, it features its own private beach, and buffet breakfast and is perfect for a romantic getaway.

Hotel Mira Mare: This modern hotel is located right in the centre and nearby to the beautiful Ksamil beaches.

GJIROKASTRA

GJIROKASTRA

The charming UNESCO town of Gjirokastra is a great destination for a night or two. You may also know Gjirokastra as the city of stone or by its Albanian name, Gjirokastër.

Unlike Berat, Gjirokastra sits on top of a hill overlooking the mountains and valley below. Gjirokaster Castle is also one of the best-preserved castles in Albania and still has many weapons which are on display today. In my eyes, Gjirokastra Castle is the best castle in Albania.

HOW TO GET TO GJIROKASTRA

You can reach Gjirokaster relatively easy from any major city or town in Albania via bus.

One thing to note is that the bus stop does not go all the way up the hill into Gjirokaster Old Town. It will drop you off at the bottom where you can either walk, catch another bus or catch a taxi to the Old Town.

In the summer, this can be quite the mission as the temperatures in Gjirokastra (and throughout Albania) are high. During those times I would definitely catch a bus/taxi up or you could even try hitchhiking, it's very popular in Albania!

THINGS TO DO

VISIT GJIROKASTER CASTLE

It's easy to get to the castle, you can either drive, catch a taxi or walk like I normally do. It's a little uphill but will only take you 5 minutes to reach from Gjirokastra Old Town. You could spend at least a couple of hours roaming around the castle.

Within Gjirokaster Castle is a weapon museum and prison too which you have to pay extra for (200 lek) but you can pick up and observe the old weapons found here. They have a lot of really useful information up there too.

Otherwise, you can roam all of the rooms, tunnels and admire the view from the top! The clock tower is a must-see which sits on the furthest side of Gjirokastra Castle from the entrance

WONDER THE GJIROKASTRA BAZAAR

Just around the corner from Gjirokaster Castle is the bazaar. One of the best things to do in Gjirokaster is wander through the bazaar and admire the architecture of the traditional buildings. There's plenty of great shopping you can do in in the bazaar too including old second-hand shops where you will find some interesting treasures!

VISIT THE ETHNOGRAPHIC MUSEUM

The old dictator of the communist period Enver Hoxha was born in Gjirokaster. Nowadays the house where he was born has been turned into a museum so you can see what a traditional Gjirokastra family home would have looked like back then.

VISIT ZEKATI FAMILY HOUSE

Another great house to visit in Gjirokaster is the Zekati House which was built in 1811-1812. This house has undergone restoration and is one of the most incredible traditional houses within Gjirokastra today. With three floors, wooden carved ceilings, two twin towers and a magnificent view of the town, this is a must-see when visiting Gjirokastra. You will want to drive or take a taxi to reach here as it's further up the hill from the bazaar.

SKENDULI HOUSE

Between Gjirokastra Castle and the Ethnographic Museum is the Skenduli House. This is another perfect example of the traditional architecture of Gjirokastra. This house was said to built around the 1700's!

THINGS TO DO

DISCOVER THE UNDERGROUND OF GJIROKASTRA

Underneath Gjirokaster Castle and Gjirokastra Old Town is an underground bunker that is now possible to explore! One of the best things to do in Gjirokastra is to visit the underground city, especially in the summer to cool off below ground. It goes down more than 80 meters deep and is over 1km long.

This underground city has over 100 rooms including interrogation rooms, offices and so on as well as multiple escape routes. This is a stark reminder of the dark communist era that loomed over Albania from 1944 until 1992.

WHERE TO EAT

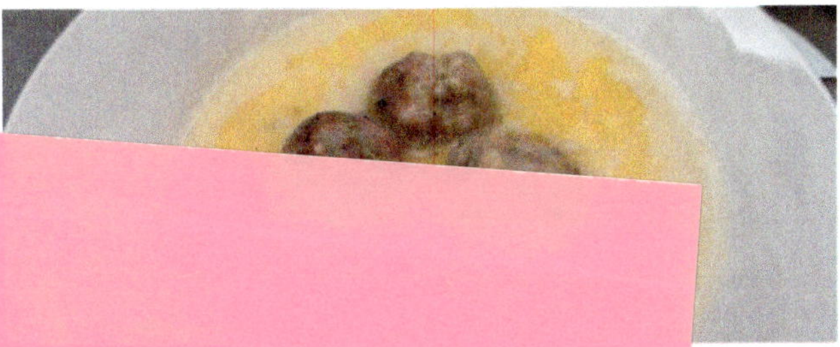

came highly
sited was not
does the best
d.

oyed the food
try!

te Gjirokaster
t in gjirokaster
but also other
us, you have to
ve tasted in the
country.

WHERE TO STAY

There are some stunning homestays and hotels in Gjirokaster where you can get an insight into the beautiful architecture within the town.

Kerculla Resort: This hotel in Gjirokastra came highly recommended by one of my readers and upon research, it's the top-rated hotel in the town. It's a beautiful hotel equipped with a swimming pool and stunning views.

Guesthouse Mele: This guesthouse is a perfect base for exploring the city of Gjirokastra. It's only a 5-10 minute walk to the old bazaar but far away enough that it's peaceful & quiet. The breakfast is fantastic and quite a spread of delicious Albanian food. The hosts of the guesthouse are the real highlight of this guesthouse though!

Hostel: The best hostel in Gjirokastra and my favourite one in Albania is **Stone City Hostel**. It's a hostel which has had some incredible renovations and is possibly the most beautiful hostel ever!

ALBANIAN FOOD TO TRY

1

TAVA E KOSIT (LAMB WITH YOGHURT)

Tava e kosit is a popular Albanian lamb dish that's baked in yoghurt. It's a simple dish which is baked with garlic, oregano and rice. The lamb is tender and flavourful and there should be a nice golden layer on the dish when it comes out of the oven

2

JANI ME FASULE (WHITE BEAN SOUP)

This is a hearty dish usually eaten in the winter to warm up the insides. It's made with white cannelloni beans, tomato paste, olive oil and onion

3

PASTICHE

This traditional Albanian dish can be described as a quiche. It's made with milk, butter, white cheese (feta) and cooked spaghetti. Then it's put all together and baked to make a slice.

4

FËRGESË

The most popular and common way is white cheese with red peppers, tomatoes, onion, a little flour, butter and yoghurt! Then it's mixed together and cooked in a clay pot in the oven. It's incredibly delicious and one I recommend having! They have variations that are spicy and one that's made with liver.

5

BYREK

You will find byrek everywhere here. It's a popular breakfast option for Albanians or a great snack on the go. But you should know there are LOTS of different flavours, combinations and textures to a byrek.

The most popular is the crispy flaky pastry stuffed with white cheese. There's also broshura which is a type of byrek that's made from greens such as spinach.

6

PERIME NË SCARË (GRILLED VEGETABLES)

Grilled vegetables are a popular complement to any Albanian dish, especially if you're having grilled meat which is also popular in Albania. Have them with a dash of balsamic vinegar and it's delicious!

7

FLEA/ FLI

This is a layered pancake dish made using a grill. It's a simple recipe but it cooks for a few hours. You keep lathering the pancakes while it's baking slowly making a delicious, soft dessert. It's usually served with some local honey or yoghurt.

8

SPECA TE MBUSHURA (PEPPER STUFFED WITH CHEESE)

Peppers are stuffed with white cheese (feta) and cooked in the oven. This dish is mouth-watering and simply delicious.

9

QOFTE

This is essentially a meatball, but longer and more delicious in my opinion. It's made with minced lamb, garlic and herbs then fried in hot oil.

10

TARATOR (COLD SOUP)

This delicious soup is made with yoghurt, garlic, thyme and vinegar. Apparently, it's good for a rough hangover. It's the perfect soup for summer, so it's also called summer soup!

11

PERSHESH

This dish is a traditional Albanian food from the city of Elbasan. It's turkey with bread and walnuts. This is a meal which you may find hard to locate in restaurants within the touristy areas.

12

PAÇE KOKE (HEAD SOUP)

Don't worry, it's the head of a lamb! This traditional Albanian food is like a meat stew. It's hearty and popular in Albania, something you would find in a typical Albanian home!

13

PACE PLENCI

This dish is like the #12 but instead of a head, it made from tripe (the insides).

14

KULAC (BREAD)

This traditional Albanian bread is firm, dense and known as soda bread. It's a great compliment to a meal and its very inexpensive.

15

KUKUREC

Another tripe inspired dish, kukurec is a grilled form of intestines and liver. The liver is wrapped in the intestines and then grilled for a grilled meat taste

16

SALCE KOSI

This is like what tzatziki is in Greece, this is a dip made from yoghurt and garlic.

17

JAPRAK (WRAPPED VINE LEAVES)

Japrak is minced lamb, rice, herbs and cooked until tender. I highly recommend tasting Japrak.

18

QIFQI (VEGETABLE RISOTTO BALLS)

This traditional Albanian food is essentially vegetable risotto balls. Egg, rice and herbs are mixed together then cooked into deep fried balls.

19

BYREK ME KUNGULL (WITH PUMPKIN)

This particular Albanian byrek is made with mashed pumpkin and its delicious. It's sort of sweet but savoury at the same time. A perfect snack or even meal!

20

QUMESHTOR (MILK PIE)

Qumeshtor is unique to Albanian food. It is basically a byrek, but you may be surprised because this one is sweet! It's made with milk, eggs and vanilla. It tastes similar to custard.

21

DJATHË I BARDHË (BAKED CHEESE)

This is exactly what the translation is, baked cheese! White cheese is also known as feta and is baked with olive oil, herbs and sometimes olives or tomato and pepper.

22

BAKLAVA

Although this isn't a traditional Albanian food (this dessert comes from Turkey), it tastes delicious and should be tried while you're travelling Albania! Baklava is a sweet dessert with layers of crispy pastry filled with honey, walnuts and many delicious things

23

PETULLA

Petulla is like little fried doughnuts or churro balls. It's usually served with honey or chocolate sauce. Along the Albanian Riviera, you will usually find people walking up and down the beaches selling these little treats!

24

SHENDETLI

This is a sweet honey biscuit cake and again, walnuts! Seems to be a popular theme with Albanian desserts.

25

KADAIF

Kadaif is a sweet and crispy Albanian dessert which looks like it has hair on top! It's also made with filo pastry like Baklava. It's simple to make. The filo pastry is shredded to make it's strange texture.

DRINKS TO TRY

1

RAKI

It's a distilled alcohol made from fruit (usually grapes but it's made form lots of other fruits too!). It's very strong, you may not be able to drink it all!

2

DHALLE

Dhalle is a sour yoghurt drink like the Turkish drink ayran. Albanians usually have this with a byrek or if you're eating something spicy then this is your best friend!

3

BOZË

This is a simple Albanian drink containing corn flour, wheat flour, sugar and water. Bozë is an ancient drink influenced by Ottomans. It's a sort of brown/yellow colour.

4

ALBANIAN BEER

You can find some local Albanian beer, the most popular being Korca which is made in the city of Korca – wow who would have thought?! They make a couple of different beers, a light and a dark.

5

EXPRESSO

Expresso is an integral part of Albanian cuisine. Did you know that Albania has the most coffee shops per capita than any other country in the world? Albanians love coffee

SOUVENIRS I RECOMMEND

CERAMICS

One of the best things to purchase for a souvenir is a homemade ceramic vase with traditional Albanian patterns. You will find some workshops around the country, but I highly recommend visiting ZadrimArt. They have a shop next to Mrizi i Zanave, which is the most famous agritourism business in Albania.

ÇIFTELI

Çifteli is a traditional instrument which can be found mostly in the north of Albania. It's a sort of guitar-like instrument with only two strings. In the traditional Albanian songs, you will hear this unique tone of the instrument.

OLIVE OIL

Albania has some of the tastiest olive oil in the world. It's fresh, delicious and has a beautiful colour to it that only the best quality olive oil has. Being so close to Italy, it's no wonder that Olive oil is of equal quality of what you can get in Italy.

QILIM

A Qilim or a handwoven rug is a fantastic souvenir that you are likely never to forget. These beautiful handwoven rugs are a favourite of mine. One of the best places to find one of these is the city of Kruja.

ART

There are some incredible artists within Albania, and you will find beautiful handmade drawings within the touristy areas. One of my favourites was a drawing I brought off a family within the castle walls of Berat.

PUPA

Pupa is one of my favourite things to buy. It is essentially hand-knitted socks that are worn over socks within a house. They are sort of like fabric slippers and are usually made by grandmothers to keep your feet toasty warm in the winter months.

Q & A

Anita answers your questions...

Since I started writing about Albania I have received a large amount of questions. Here are my most popular questions with answers!

Q HOW DO I GET A SIM CARD?

If you would like to get a sim card you can do so at any of the Vodafone shops around. There's one at the airport if you fly into Tirana. They will get you set up on a local sim fast and easily.

For under €10 you can get 5MB of data with calling & texting.

Q CAN YOU DRINK THE WATER IN ALBANIA?

I wouldn't recommend drinking the water in Albania. The water throughout the country has high levels of chloride and heavy metals. I used to drink the water myself but noticed after a couple of months I started to experience bad stomach pains.

Then, I found that none of the locals drink the water, that's when you know not to drink it!

Q HOW'S THE WIFI IN ALBANIA?

Believe it or not, I have found Albania to have better Wi-Fi than in New Zealand. It's fast and reliable.

As I now live in Albania, I have a Wi-Fi router which was free to set up and cost me 2000 lek per month. Most accommodation options and restaurants will have Wi-Fi.

Q HOW DO I FIND A LONG-TERM RENTAL IN ALBANIA?

Not online, by networking! To find the best apartment for the best price you have to come to Albania first and ask as many of the locals as you can. If you book online beforehand then you will most likely be paying double.

Also, if you're looking for a long-term rental specifically in Saranda then don't come in July and August as the prices rise due to these being the busiest months. If you want to know the best groups to join then flick to the 'Moving to Albania' section of this guide.

WHAT'S IT' LIKE BUYING A HOUSE/APARTMENT IN ALBANIA?

Due to having no personal experience myself of buying a house here I can't really comment. However, I have heard that the number one thing you need to make sure of when purchasing any house or land here is to get the official documents.

After communism fell, most of the land was taken over by whoever wants it. There are still many land disputes to this day as many houses don't have official papers.

WHERE ARE THE AIRPORTS?

There's only one international airport in Tirana for now but they are building another in Vlore (south Albania) which should be open in a few years.

DOES ALBANIA HAVE A HIGH POLLUTION RATE?

I am not sure of the official statistics for this, but I guess it depends where you are situated. If you are living in Tirana, then pollution is going to be higher because you are in a city with a lot of traffic etc. If you're in a city like Saranda then it's going to be less because it's quieter.

HOW DO I GET AROUND IN ALBANIA?

The best way is by car if you want to explore the likes of the Albanian Riviera so you can stop over at all the hidden beaches and coves. You have to watch other people's driving though and road rules are simply just suggestions to Albanians. There are also buses and furgons (small buses), which are usually reliable but sometimes the timetables change so it's best to ask the locals about bus times.

WHAT'S THE EASIEST WAY TO GET TO ALBANIA FROM ELSEWHERE IN EUROPE?

It totally depends where in Albania you want to start. If you want to start in Tirana, then you can fly into the airport. They are also building another airport in Vlore which should be open in the next few years. There are also a lot of buses coming from Montenegro, Kosovo, Macedonia, and Greece.

If you want to start in Saranda (the south) then the best option is to fly into Corfu, Greece which is an island not far from Saranda. It takes a 30-minute ferry ride and is the best way to get to here from the UK as EasyJet offer very affordable flights to and from Corfu.

WHAT ARE YOUR FAVOURITE PLACES IN ALBANIA?

My favourite region – The Albanian Riviera! Beautiful beaches, delicious food and lots of sunshine!

More specifically, I love Saranda, Dhermi, Himare, and Borsh!

IS ALBANIA SAFE TO VISIT?

Yes, Albania is safe to visit. Despite the cat calling from men sometimes, it is safe for foreigners and women travelling alone.

I have travelled around Albania mostly by myself and have never had a problem

IS ALBANIA GOOD FOR A DIGITAL NOMAD?

Yes, absolutely! Albania is incredible affordable for digital nomads. there is talks that Albania might be introducing a digital nomad visa in the future which will make it easier!

Does Albania accept Euro and/or USD

Yes, sometimes. Most places will accept euros, but not USD. To avoid any confusion, I would recommend to keep Lek on you at all times.

PACKING CHECKLIST

Here's your ultimate Albania packing list so you don't forget anything important!

Spring/Summer

MUST-HAVES

- Passport
- Travel insurance
- Visa documents
- Lek or Euro

CLOTHING

- Bathing suit
- Dresses/skirts/shorts
- Tank tops/t-shirts
- Light jumper
- Sandals
- Flip flops
- Water shoes
- Lightweight jacket
- Sunglasses
- Sunhat
- Sneakers

BEAUTY/HEALTH

- Sunscreen
- Toothpaste/Toothbrush
- Hairbrush
- Razor
- Lotion
- Makeup
- Deodorant
- Vitamins
- Medication
- Feminine hygiene products

PACKING

- Travel backpack/suitcase
- Packing cubes
- Quick drying towel
- Laundry kit
- Umbrella

TECH

- Headphones
- Battery pack
- Phone + Charger
- Laptop + Charger
- Camera
- SD cards
- Kindle

MISCELLANEOUS

- Canvas Tote
- Laundry bag
- Water bottle
- Notebook/Journal
- Padlock

PACKING CHECKLIST

Autumn/Winter

MUST-HAVES

- [ ] Passport
- [ ] Travel insurance
- [ ] Visa documents
- [ ] Lek or Euro

CLOTHING

- [ ] Beanie / Warm Hat
- [ ] Gloves
- [ ] T-shirts / Long-sleeve tops
- [ ] Thick jumper
- [ ] Pants/ Jeans / Leggings
- [ ] Scarf
- [ ] Thermal clothing
- [ ] Jacket
- [ ] Sunglasses
- [ ] Boots
- [ ] Sneakers

BEAUTY/HEALTH

- [ ] Sunscreen
- [ ] Toothpaste/Toothbrush
- [ ] Hairbrush
- [ ] Razor
- [ ] Lotion
- [ ] Makeup
- [ ] Deodorant
- [ ] Vitamins
- [ ] Medication
- [ ] Feminine hygiene products

PACKING

- [ ] Travel backpack/suitcase
- [ ] Packing cubes
- [ ] Quick drying towel
- [ ] Laundry kit
- [ ] Umbrella

TECH

- [ ] Headphones
- [ ] Battery pack
- [ ] Phone + Charger
- [ ] Laptop + Charger
- [ ] Camera
- [ ] SD cards
- [ ] Kindle

MISCELLANEOUS

- [ ] Canvas Tote
- [ ] Laundry bag
- [ ] Water bottle
- [ ] Notebook/Journal
- [ ] Padlock

MOVING TO ALBANIA

Moving to Albania was one of the best decisions I ever made, and I encourage others to do the same if they can. But like anywhere, living in Albania has pros and cons, so I have included some of the downsides, as well!

WHY I CHOSE TO LIVE IN ALBANIA

I fell in love with Albania in March 2017 when I took an overnight road trip with some people I met in a hostel in Kotor, Montenegro. We decided on a spontaneous trip to Albania. By the time we got to the north of Albania – Shkodër it was late afternoon. We checked into our hostel and for €5 we got a bed, a beer, and a free breakfast, I couldn't believe it. It was almost like we had transported ourselves to Asia where the prices are incredibly low.

We then went out for a meal we ordered a table full of different dishes plus wine and it cost no more than €6 or €7 each. What was this place?

If you haven't already noticed Albania's prices are crazy cheap compared to the rest of Europe, especially for tourists. A hostel will cost you next to nothing and so will your meals. It's the perfect place if you want to explore somewhere that's affordable. And it isn't just visiting, the general cost of living in Albania is lower than in most of Europe. This is not the only reason I chose to move to Albania, but it definitely was a big advantage!

IS LIVING IN ALBANIA SAFE?

This is probably the number one question I get asked about Albanian life. There are a lot of misconceptions about Albania and its safety. Albania is not full of gangsters, sex traffickers and mafia walking around on the streets. Every country in this world has its share of bad people but living in Albania, I haven't met any yet. I feel safer living and travelling here than in most western European countries. The tourist crime rate here is very low.

Albania also has a code of Besa which is the highest ethical code and roughly translates to 'to keep the promise'. Albanians are very loyal people and if they see tourists they feel it is their duty to keep them safe and feel welcomed. For these reasons, I have never felt unsafe living in Albania.

DISADVANTAGES OF MOVING TO ALBANIA

As I said before, living in Albania comes with both pros and cons. There have definitely been struggles with moving to Albania. In addition to my visa process, another downside is that food is very limited in variety. You will find an abundance of Greek food, Italian and obviously Albanian food but if you're craving something spicy, you're going to be hard-pressed to find one unless you're in Tirana. But I feel like that's a small price to pay to live in such an untouched and beautifully raw destination like Albania.

Albanian life is slow-paced and relaxed and it's probably my favourite place I have lived in so far as it's so different from anything I have experienced. There are even a number of ex-pats who come to retire in Albania. Tirana and Saranda are popular choices for ex-pats who move to Albania, although it is of course possible to live elsewhere. Living in Albania is a great option for old and young

HOW TO FIND AN APARTMENT

If you would like to find an apartment in Albania, I would recommend joining the various expats groups for Albania. Here you can ask if anyone has apartment recommendations. This is how a majority of expats find apartments in Albania. Here are some of the best ones to join:

Expats in Albania
Expats in Saranda
Expats in Tirana
Expats and Albanians in Durres
Expats in Vlora

GETTING A VISA

If you are moving to Albania, you will most likely need a visa, but obviously, this depends on which country you are from. If you are from the US, you get 1 year visa-free.

When you come to Albania, and you're planning to stay long-term, I highly recommend visiting your local immigration office so you can ask directly what you need and what your options are.

RESOURCES

BOOKING.COM

The most popular accommodation booking site for Albania

HOSTELWORLD

#1 booking site for hostels in Albania

TRUSTED HOUSESITTERS

Travel & look after pets around the world

VIATOR

#1 recommendation for tours around Albania

WORLD NOMADS

Travel insurance perfect for digital nomads & frequent travellers

SAFETY WING

Travel insurance recommendation that starts as low as $42 for 4 weeks!

TRAVELLING ALBANIA

Have you joined our Facebook community with over 2000 members? Search for '**Travelling Albania**' on Facebook to connect with like-minded travellers and have your questions answered in real time!

UPGRADE!

If you liked this guide then upgrade to gain access to my other two digital products.

40-PAGE BUCKETLIST E-BOOK

40 unbelievable things to do in Albania Ebook is a 40-page bucket list that includes my absolute top recommendations for any traveller coming to Albania. Think of it as your ultimate Albania bucket list!

Get it at: https://bit.ly/36NvFOa

ALBANIA ITINERARY PACK

The itinerary pack includes 5 itinerary samples for your trip including 5 days, 1 week, 10 days, 2 weeks & 1 month. These can be adjusted depending on your wants + needs!

Get it at: https://bit.ly/2UYwf96

Thank you

Thank you so much for supporting my mission to bring more people aware of the beauty of Albania. Your support means the world to me!

Anita Hendrieka

TRAVEL BLOGGER

WWW.ANITAHENDRIEKA.COM

COPYRIGHT DISCLAIMER

Printed in Great Britain
by Amazon

43193141R00099